D1375624

Transparency in Financial Reporting

LANCHESTER LIBRARY, Coventry University
Gosford Street, Coventry CVI 5DD Telephone 024 7688 7555

WITHDRAWN

Lanchester Library

This book is due to be returned not later than the date and
time stamped above. Fines are charged on overdue books

HARRIMAN HOUSE LTD

3A Penns Road
Petersfield
Hampshire
GU32 2EW
GREAT BRITAIN

Tel: +44 (0)1730 233870
Fax: +44 (0)1730 233880
Email: enquiries@harriman-house.com
Website: www.harriman-house.com

First published in Great Britain in 2009

Copyright © Harriman House Ltd

The right of Ruth Ann McEwen to be identified as the author has been asserted
in accordance with the Copyright, Design and Patents Act 1988.

ISBN13 978-1-906659-13-4

British Library Cataloguing in Publication Data
A CIP catalogue record for this book can be obtained from the British Library.

All rights reserved; no part of this publication may be reproduced, stored in a retrieval
system, or transmitted in any form or by any means, electronic, mechanical,
photocopying, recording, or otherwise without the prior written permission of the
Publisher. This book may not be lent, resold, hired out or otherwise disposed of by
way of trade in any form of binding or cover other than that in which it is published
without the prior written consent of the Publisher.

Printed and bound by the CPI Antony Rowe, Chippenham.

No responsibility for loss occasioned to any person or corporate body acting or
refraining to act as a result of reading material in this book can be accepted by
the Publisher, by the Author, or by the employer of the Author.

Coventry University Library

Contents

For SAM

About the author

Ruth Ann McEwen is Associate Dean of Accreditation and Administration and Professor of Accounting for the Sawyer Business School at Suffolk University. She earned her Ph.D. in Industrial Management with a concentration in Accounting from the Georgia Institute of Technology and taught Financial Accounting at the Master's and Doctoral levels for more than 20 years. She is the author or co-author of more than 40 refereed articles and proceedings focusing on the usefulness of accounting information. She has published in such premier journals as *The Accounting Review*, *Decision Sciences*, *Accounting Horizons*, *CPA Journal*, *International Journal of Accounting* and the *Journal of Business Ethics* and is the author of "Earnings Per Share" and co-author of "Asset Retirement Obligations" published by Tax Management, Inc. In 1998, she presented a series of research papers to a joint seminar of the Financial Accounting Standards Board (FASB) and the Governmental Accounting Standards Board (GASB) focusing on current financial reporting.

From 2005 until 2008, Ruth Ann McEwen served as a consultant to the FASB, authorized as a content expert to codify United States Generally Accepted Accounting Principles (US GAAP), which comprises authoritative guidance for US corporate financial reporting. She has received numerous scholarly, teaching and research awards.

Introduction

By January 1, 2012, all major economies will provide financial reports using International Financial Reporting Standards (IFRS) except for Argentina, Greenland, parts of Africa and the United States. While the US Securities and Exchange Commission (SEC) recently published a roadmap for transition from US GAAP to IFRS, the roadmap does not include an irrevocable transition date; instead, mandatory adoption will depend on accomplishing objectives represented by milestones. It is likely that these objectives will be met and transition will occur by 2016. This work will set out the key differences between IFRS and US GAAP from a practitioner's perspective, although financial analysts also will benefit from the material presented. The work identifies issues related to potential adoption of IFRS in the US and is aimed at intermediate to advanced practitioners and analysts.

IFRS differs in many respects from US GAAP, but no difference is as substantive as the IFRS view that all assets and liabilities can be revalued to fair value each reporting period, implicitly suggesting that only one value is "fair" and that managers are able to measure it. Unlike IFRS, US GAAP recognizes assets and liabilities at cost and, in most cases, revaluation reflects only decreases in value.

Balance sheet items are shown net of adjustments that keep assets from being overstated and liabilities from being understated. Alternately, assets and liabilities under IFRS are revalued each period to reflect both increases and decreases in value. Under both US GAAP and IFRS, decreases in value lead to unrealized losses that are recognized into current earnings or equity. Under IFRS and in fewer circumstances under US GAAP, increases in value lead to unrealized gains that may be recognized into current earnings. Recognition of these unrealized (no transition has occurred) holding gains may seriously inflate measures of earnings and income.

IFRS, and in certain circumstances US GAAP, is viewed by some as providing useful information for investors and creditors because of the fair value requirement. Under either system, revaluation methods may be straightforward or extremely obscure. An example of a straightforward method would be revaluing a building at a price for similar buildings in a similar area in a functioning real estate market. But most revaluations are not straightforward.

More obscure methods employ pricing models based on unobservable inputs in markets that are not fully functioning. For example, consider the case of fair valuation of a contingent consideration acquired as part of a business combination. Recognition and periodic revaluation requires estimates of the cash flows associated with the contingency (usually based on a subjective probability distribution) and the choice of an appropriate discount rate reflecting the risk of the acquired entity. Depending on the nature of the consideration, active markets may not exist. Both IFRS and US GAAP require the consideration to be recognized at fair value and that its estimates and managerial judgments be disclosed. But even with extensive disclosure about cash flow estimates and risk analysis, additional disclosure does not guarantee greater transparency or enhanced usefulness of the financial information being presented.

The financial crisis which began in 2008 has been attributed to, among other things, a perceived lack of transparency in the financial markets. In general, transparency implies an ability to see the reported results of an entity's financial activities clearly and to use these results in making investment decisions. At question is the belief that transparency in financial reporting will lead to transparency in financial markets. Unfortunately, this link may be more subjective than most of us wish.

This book presents an analysis of reporting issues affecting transparency under IFRS, compared with US GAAP, and suggests areas of concern for preparers and users of financial reports. I also provide a technical analysis of major accounting issues raised by convergence, and indicate areas of interest during initial adoption of IFRS by US entities.

Part One

Transparency of Financial Reporting

In recent years, the transparency debate has largely focused on US GAAP and whether its proper application could offset Wall Street greed. Many believe that even with proper application, US accounting principles are too complex and proscriptive, and result in a system in which entities tend to follow form over substance while violating the underlying spirit of transparency. IFRS guidelines focus on broader principles and give entities more leeway to reflect those principles. Managers are provided with guidance that encourages reporting which reflects the true underlying substance of financial transactions. There is an expectation that convergence of US GAAP and IFRS will take the best practices of rules-based and principles-based accounting standards, resulting in the highest quality financial reporting possible. Under such a setting, transparency would be greatly enhanced.

1. Transparency and Financial Reporting Quality

Transparency may be viewed as a financial reporting quality indicator. While a single definition of financial reporting quality does not exist, markets have described a similar construct: earnings quality. Some view higher quality earnings as being more 'persistent.'[1] Others suggest current earnings quality should be defined for shareholders who rely on financial reports to buy future earnings.[2] All definitions seem to extend the idea that higher quality earnings are those that enable higher quality decisions about the future prospects for an entity.[3] Market based

---

[1] Scott Richardson, "Earnings Quality and Short Sellers", *Accounting Horizons* 17, Supplement (2003), pp. 49-61.

[2] Stephen H. Penman, "The Quality of Financial Statements: Perspectives from the Recent Stock Market Bubble", *Accounting Horizons* 17, Supplement (2003), pp. 77-96.

[3] Katherine Schipper and Linda Vincent, "Earnings Quality", *Accounting Horizons* 17, Supplement (2003), pp. 97-110.

definitions of earnings quality relate higher quality to the ability of a firm to generate cash[4] or to be useful in predicting the future, as summarized in the following quote published in the *CPA Journal* in 2005:

> Earnings quality refers to the ability of reported earnings to reflect the company's true earnings, as well as the usefulness of reported earnings to predict future earnings. Earnings quality also refers to the stability, persistence, and lack of variability in reported earnings.[5]

High-quality earnings can be characterized as 'repeatable, controllable and bankable.'[6] In general, 'taken as a whole, the quality of earnings can generally be summarized as the degree to which earnings are cash or non-cash, recurring or nonrecurring, and based on precise measurement or estimates that are subject to change.'[7] Alternately, diminished earnings quality has been described as, 'the extent to which net income reported on the income statement differs from true earnings.'[8]

Note that some definitions seemingly conflict with others. Predictable earnings may be useful in predicting future earnings streams, but may not reflect the underlying volatility of an entity's transactions. For example, entities with seasonal earnings patterns may be more difficult to predict, but the quality of earnings may be quite high. Persistent or recurring earnings as a determinant of earnings quality seems to be

---

[4] www.ratefinancials.com

[5] Jodi L. Bellovary, Don E. Giacomino, and Michael D. Akers, "Earnings Quality: It's Time to Measure and Report", www.nysscpa.org/cpajournal/2005/1105/essentials/p32.htm.

[6] www.investopedia.com/articles/02/103002.asp

[7] Deloitte & Touche, *Quality of Earnings*, 2002.

8 Frank Hodge, "Investors' Perceptions of Earnings Quality, Auditor Independence, and the Usefulness of Audited Financial Information", *Accounting Horizons* 17, Supplement (2003), pp. 37-48.

straightforward, but upon deeper examination, persistence implies the potential for smoothing, which is in conflict with the idea of having current earnings reflect an entity's true earnings.

Under US GAAP, the underlying objective of financial reporting is to provide information that is useful to decision makers, primarily investors, in predicting the future earnings and cash flows of an entity. For financial statements to be useful to decision makers they must be transparent and of high quality – in other words, they must be representationally faithful.[9] Higher quality financial reports exhibit a high degree of correspondence between what they measure and what they purport to measure.[10] The AICPA notes that true earnings quality underlies the relation between the economic substance of a transaction, and our ability to reflect the transaction using accounting rules that require substantive judgment in a world of increasingly complex rules and transactions.[11] Transparency represents the next layer of the financial reporting model. Transparent financial reports are clear, accurate reports that reflect the economic substance of transactions in a straightforward manner, even in times of great uncertainty.

---

[9] See Schipper and Vincent, "Earnings Quality", Supplement, *Accounting Horizons* (2003), pp. 97-110 for a discussion of Earnings Quality.

[10] CON 2, ¶ 63.

[11] http://fmcenter.aicpa.org/Resources/Traditional/Quality+of+Earnings+Case+Study+Collection.htm

2. Transparency of the Balance Sheet: Fair Valuation

A. Fair valuation under alternative market assumptions

Much of the current controversy regarding full adoption of IFRS for US GAAP entities rests on the relation between fair valuation and financial reporting transparency. International Accounting Standard No. 18 (IAS 18) defines fair value as, 'the amount for which an asset could be exchanged, or a liability settled, between knowledgeable, willing parties in an arm's length transaction.'[12] FASB's Codification[13] Master Glossary provides two similar definitions, stating that fair value represents, 'the amount at which an asset (or liability) could be bought (or incurred) or sold (or settled) in a current transaction between willing parties, that is, other than in a forced or liquidation sale,' and 'the price that would be received to sell an asset or paid to transfer a liability in an orderly transaction between market participants at the measurement date.' The first FASB definition was introduced as part of CON 7 and the second was provided in FAS 157. Note that these definitions imply active participants with available market prices.

But how are assets and liabilities valued if market prices are not available? FAS 107 identifies alternatives:

> Quoted market prices, if available, are the best evidence of the fair value of financial instruments. If quoted market prices are not available, management's best estimate of fair value may be based on the quoted market price of a financial instrument with similar characteristics or on valuation techniques (for

---

[12] IAS 18, ¶ 7.

[13] Note that subsequent sections of this book will discuss FASB's Codification project and the terminology which will be required to reference authoritative guidance after July 1, 2009.

example, the present value of estimated future cash flows using a discount rate commensurate with the risks involved, option pricing models or matrix pricing models).

FAS 157 identifies three valuation techniques that are to be consistently applied in estimating fair value:

1   The market approach uses prices and other relevant information generated by market transactions involving identical or comparable assets or liabilities;

2   The income approach uses valuation techniques (including present value techniques, option-pricing models such as the Black-Scholes-Merton formula, and the multi-period excess earnings method which reflects a discounted cash flow method used to estimate the fair value of certain intangible assets) to convert future amounts, for example, cash flows or earnings, to a single present discounted amount;

3   The cost approach which is based on the amount that currently would be required to replace the service capacity of an asset (often referred to as current replacement cost).

B. Hierarchy of inputs

In addition, FAS 157 establishes a revised hierarchy of inputs to be used in determining fair value estimates. Comparable to FAS 107, the hierarchy gives the highest priority to observable market inputs and the lowest priority to unobservable market inputs as follows:

- Level 1 inputs are quoted prices (unadjusted) in active markets for identical assets or liabilities that the reporting entity has the ability to access at the measurement date;

- Level 2 inputs are inputs other than quoted prices included within Level 1 that are observable for the asset or liability, either directly or indirectly;

- Level 3 inputs are unobservable inputs for the asset or liability, (e.g. inputs derived through extrapolation or interpolation that cannot be corroborated by observable market data).

Level 1 inputs transparently reflect fair value. Fair valuation of either financial or non-financial assets based on recent sales for identical assets in functioning markets conveys the underlying true value of the assets and reflects the substance of fair valuation as promulgated by IFRS. The same can be said for non-financial or financial liabilities using Level 1 inputs: such comparisons communicate the underlying outflow required to settle the liability and they fairly reflect the intent of periodic revaluation.

Level 2 inputs include:

(a) quoted prices for similar assets or liabilities in active markets;

(b) quoted prices for identical or similar assets or liabilities in markets that are not active;

(c) inputs other than quoted prices that are observable for the asset or liability (e.g. interest rates and yield curves observable at commonly quoted intervals, volatilities, prepayment speeds, loss severities, credit risks, and default rates);

(d) inputs that are derived principally from or corroborated by observable market data by correlation or other means (market-corroborated inputs). Level 2 inputs are more problematic. Use of "similar" prices invariably leads to subjectivity in determining exactly which prices are similar to the asset or liability being revalued. While current US GAAP requires extensive subjectivity,

Level 2 estimation exacerbates what is already a well documented problem in US financial reporting: understatement of risk and manipulation of earnings.

Level 3 inputs should be used to measure fair value to the extent that observable inputs are not available, thereby allowing for situations in which there is little, if any, market activity for the asset or liability. However, FAS 157's emphasis that the fair value objective in Level 3 continues to be an exit price from the perspective of a market participant may diminish transparency and certainly increases the complexity of the financial statements.

Under the guidance of FAS 157, entities must estimate these inputs not from an internal perspective, but from the view of an external party who would exchange for the asset, or assume the liability, at a fair price reflecting appropriate risk levels. The guidance provided by FAS 157 seems to suggest that external markets could or would price the risk of an asset retirement obligation in 2010 to decommission a nuclear power plant in 2030 and that an external party would be willing to assume the risk.

FAS 157 uses the term 'inputs' to refer broadly to the assumptions that market participants would use in pricing the asset or liability, including assumptions about risk. It indicates that valuation techniques should maximize the use of observable inputs (Levels 1 and 2) and minimize the use of unobservable inputs (Level 3). Observable inputs are those that reflect assumptions market participants would use in pricing the asset or liability developed, based on market data obtained from sources independent of the reporting entity. Unobservable inputs are inputs that reflect the reporting entity's own assumptions about the *assumptions* (emphasis added) market participants would use in pricing the asset or liability developed based on the best information available in the circumstances.[14] Valuation under the Level 3 provisions of FAS 157 is based not on entity-specific estimates, but on estimates of what external parties would estimate. This uncertainty seems counterintuitive and is likely to diminish transparency.

C. Hierarchy of inputs: example

For example, assume that an entity must value an asset or liability using Level 3 inputs in a mathematical model. If a model such as present value is used, the entity must estimate:

(a) future cash flows,

(b) the variability in timing and amount of cash flows under differing circumstances and the likelihood of those circumstances,

(c) the price that marketplace participants demand for bearing the uncertainty inherent in those cash flows, and

(d) the time value of money.

In determining these components, value is defined by the assumptions about estimated cash flows that the external parties would make. Level 3 inputs, then, require extensive estimates based on externally-based estimates.

Consider valuation for contingent consideration under US GAAP and IFRS (FAS 141R and IFRS 3R). In certain settings, both require initial recognition at acquisition of the consideration at fair value and both require remeasurement at each reporting date until the contingency is resolved. Under US GAAP, fair value must reflect markets while IFRS entities may use entity-specific estimates. Thus, if Smith Company enters into a purchase agreement in which an earn-out clause will net

---

[14] FAS 157, paragraph 21.

Brown Company a $5 million payment and 5% of net sales for Product A contingent upon successfully defending a patent, then, at the acquisition date, Smith Company must estimate the fair value of the contingent liability. The fair value of the contingency is based on estimates of the likelihood that the defence will be successful and estimates of the cash flows from future sales of Product A.

Under FAS 157, Smith should maximize the use of observable inputs when possible. In the current setting, estimating the liability requires Smith to estimate a subjective probability distribution for each of a series of questions addressing the likelihood of defending the patent and estimates of future cash flows. For example, Smith might estimate: (1) the probability of defending the patent, (2) market sales once the patent issue has been resolved, (3) the probability that Product A will become technologically obsolete, and (4) the probability that future patent actions may reduce sales.

Smith must then use these probability weighted estimates in estimating future cash flows associated with Product A. Brown Company risks are included in the expected value of the cash flows. Since the earn-out will occur over several years, Smith must discount the expected cash flows by a risk adjusted discount rate. One choice for this rate might be the industry weighted average cost of capital. The liability would be the probability weighted cash flows (expected values) discounted at an industry cost of capital. Smith would need to remeasure the contingent liability at each reporting date.

D. Entity-specific estimates

CON 7 offers justification for using entity-specific estimates. Entities might expect to realize or pay cash flows that differ from those expected by external parties if:

(a) the entity's managers might intend different use or settlement than that anticipated by others;

(b) the entity's managers may prefer to accept risk of a liability (like a product warranty) and manage it internally, rather than transferring that liability to another party;

(c) the entity might hold special preferences, like tax or zoning variances, not available to others;

(d) the entity might hold information, trade secrets, or processes that allow it to realize (or avoid paying) cash flows that differ from others' expectations;

(e) the entity might be able to realize or pay amounts through use of internal resources.

US GAAP does not allow entity-specific measurement. US entities rely extensively on mathematical models, some of which are extremely complex with subjective estimates that can introduce extreme volatility. Take, for example, the Black-Scholes model for estimating the value of employee share based payments.[15] Under the Black-Scholes model, estimates are required for the risk-free rate and the expected volatility of common stock. These estimates are considered to remain constant over the option's term (not necessarily the case) and assumptions inherent in initial estimates can substantively affect the expense

---

[15] Black, Fischer and Myron Scholes, "The Pricing of Options and Corporate Liabilities", *The Journal of Political Economy* 81:3 (May-June 1973), pp. 637-654.

associated with the options, thus affecting income. For example, a Black-Scholes valuation of call options with an exercise price of $20 per share, a stock price at the date of the grant of $20 per share, an expected life of the option of 5 years, and no dividends would be $6.07 if the initial estimates of the risk-free rate and volatility are 6.5% and 15%, respectively. If the initial estimates are 5.0% and 10%, respectively, the valuation is reduced to $4.67, a reduction of 23% in employee compensation expense. Note that the Black-Scholes model requires assumptions that options are freely traded and that the option life is relatively short term. Neither of these assumptions is true for employee share-based payments, but the model is considered to be robust to violations of its assumptions.

IFRS does allow entity-specific estimates and requires extensive disclosure about cash flows and other fair value estimates, especially when entity-specific measures have been used. Entities may well publish the assumptions underlying their estimates in the notes to the financial statements. However, predicting volatility in markets that are not fully functioning is an uncertain task. Thus, fair valuation even with extensive disclosure may not enhance usefulness or meet the objectives of transparency. And since remeasurement gains and losses are recognized directly into income, slight changes in estimates hold the potential to affect earnings. Current accounting research suggests that valuation based on standards that are unstructured or less transparent, such as Level 3 unobservable inputs, provides a setting where managers are likely to manipulate earnings.[16] In applying that technique an entity's assumptions should be realistic; however, US GAAP guidance allows considerable latitude in estimating Level 3 unobservable inputs.

---

[16] J. Hunton, R. Libby, C. Mazza, "Financial reporting transparency and earnings management" *The Accounting Review* 81, pp. 135-157.

Such discretion calls into question the effects of fair valuation inherent in the asset/liability approach on transparency and quality of financial reporting. McInnes and Cataldo (2007) offer a particularly stinging criticism of the asset/liability approach. They state:

> Many otherwise well informed accounting and finance professionals seem unaware of the radical impact that fair value would have on our financial reporting system. According to the fair value vision, the entire framework of transaction-based accrual accounting would be replaced by a system that measures every asset and liability at an estimate of its current "fair value." Traditional concepts of revenue, expense, and matching have no place in this vision. What we currently understand as "net income" would be redefined as the change in book equity – that is, the difference between the estimated fair values of assets and liabilities, adjusted for primary capital flows. This system of comprehensive fair value accounting is known as the asset-liability approach.[17]

Noting that historic cost may be of greater use than fair value in predicting future cash flows, especially with the advent of more principles-based IFRS, McInnes and Cataldo (2007) reiterate the assertions of numerous critics of fair value accounting:

> The adoption of full fair value accounting for all assets and liabilities and convergence with IFRS will present challenges for preparers and users alike, perhaps with little benefit, and with the nontrivial possibility of great harm.

---

[17] M. McInnes and J. Cataldo, "SFAS 159: The Fair Value Option", *The CPA Journal*, August 2007, http://findarticles.com/p/articles/mi_qa5346/is_200708/ai_n21293122/pg_1.

Part Two

Financial Reporting under IFRS Convergence

While transparency has generally focused on US GAAP, the planned convergence of US GAAP with standards provided by the IASB offers a unique opportunity to view transparency of financial reporting from two perspectives. US GAAP is often viewed as overly prescriptive, while standards promulgated by IASB are considered to be based more on general principles. Neither perspective necessarily guarantees transparency.

Convergence is being viewed as one method by which asset and liability reporting will be enhanced. The effects on earnings or comprehensive income have yet to be identified. Joint committees are examining differences between IFRS and US GAAP and selecting the reporting methods considered to yield higher quality results. Smaller reporting issues may be successfully resolved in this manner. More fundamental issues, especially relating to the propensity of US accountants to generate voluminous rules in order to reduce audit liability, are expected to generate much more controversy during the convergence process.

3. Legal Basis of US GAAP and IFRS

A. Common law versus code law

Fundamental differences exist between US GAAP and the accounting rules of other countries. US GAAP consists of rules that are independently created, are considered to be "best practices" and serve as the basis for litigation. US GAAP as promulgated by FASB can be copyrighted and must be purchased by users.[18] Rappeport (2008)

---

[18] See Rappeport, "One Standard, Many Laws", *CFO* April 2008, pp. 41-42 for a discussion of the contrast between the proprietary US GAAP system, and the systems of other countries.

suggests that much of the basis for US GAAP is the common-law system modeled after that of Great Britain. Alternately, numerous other countries model accounting standards on civil law in which the standards are incorporated into a code of law and are freely distributed. Code law is created by the government and is enforced through governmental penalties.

FASB's recent codification of accounting standards[19] into a single code notwithstanding, US GAAP is common law and is considered by some to be the superior method of standardizing accounting rules. Under common law, the standards can be changed by standard setters with oversight by governmental agencies without the time consuming and political inconsistencies attributed to code law based standards. Common law penalties are exacted by shareholders in the form of litigation. Common law based standards are considered to be more transparent, are revised in a more timely manner and are more market-oriented.[20]

Code law standards, on the other hand, require a change in law to change the standard. Considering that IFRS governs the accounting standards of numerous countries with differing accounting laws, it would seem likely that complete convergence is impossible. "Carve-outs", or arbitrary changes to the standards, seem inevitable. The idea that US GAAP and IFRS will completely converge and that all users will be reporting under identical standards seems somewhat idealistic.

---

[19] www.fasb.org/news/nr011508.shtml.

[20] Id.

B. The codification

Current accounting standards in the US are extremely detailed. Prior to FASB's codification of accounting standards, a US GAAP hierarchy of sometimes conflicting and inconsistent rules enabled users to potentially manage the system by interpretation. For example, prior to the codification, Statements of Financial Accounting Standards included a section entitled, "Basis for Conclusion" in which FASB provided detailed discussion of issues raised by constituents in drafting the standard. While FASB has always stated that the basis section was non-authoritative, users have implemented reporting processes based, at least in part, on language provided in the basis section. In a similar manner, Emerging Issue Task Force consensus opinions (EITFs) are authoritative; however, EITF issues with recommendations but without a consensus are non-authoritative. Users have, in some circumstances, misunderstood or misused the distinction.

FASB's codification of accounting standards into a single code should eliminate misunderstandings about whether literature is authoritative or non-authoritative. Beginning in July 2009, the codified text will be the only source of authoritative GAAP in the US.[21] Codified standards that have resulted from recent cooperative efforts between US GAAP and IFRS standards setters are almost identical. For example, FAS 128, *Earnings per Share* is almost identical to IAS 33. Both standards were written with the idea that one standard would govern this issue and FASB and the IASB would be completely convergent on this issue. However, numerous other issues will require additional convergence efforts to ensure substantially full convergence. For example, standards

---

[21] See R. A. McEwen, T. Hoey and J. Brozovsky, "Codification: A Crucial Step Toward Simplification" *Accounting Horizons*, 20:4 (2006), pp. 391-398.

setters must still agree on financial statement presentation, financial instruments, leases, revenue recognition, fair valuation, post retirement, and a common conceptual framework.

4. Fundamental Similarities and Differences

Though standard setters have consistently worked to produce identical US GAAP and IFRS standards, fundamental differences still exist. For example, under IFRS, financial statements must meet the needs of a variety of users, including tax authorities. Under US GAAP, financial reporting must be useful to investors, creditors and others in predicting future cash flows. Since the US Tax Code can be at odds with financial reporting under US GAAP, tax authorities are not considered to be as important in US GAAP.

Both FASB and IASB are deeply involved in fair value measurement issues. In the 1990s, use of earnings per share as the most important indicator of corporate performance was associated with short-term earnings per share incentive managerial contracts, leading to short-term earnings maximization and earnings management, an unwanted and potentially illegal outcome. Under this system, the definition of assets and liabilities was not central to performance reporting. With adoption of IFRS and a fair value balance sheet, earnings and earnings per share may no longer lead performance indicators as the metric of choice in analyzing financial performance; instead, the statement of financial position and the statement of equity will be of the primary statements used to convey this information.

Differences between US GAAP and IFRS have also been caused by the codification project initiated by FASB in the early 2000s. Under US GAAP, guidance is either authoritative or not and as of July 1, 2009 the codification will be the sole source of authoritative literature.

However, under IFRS, a hierarchy still exists, suggesting the ability for countries to carve-out sections of IFRS which they don't intend to follow. Under the IFRS hierarchy, IFRS and related interpretations are considered to be the most authoritative guidance. If guidance is not directly applicable, managers are to use judgment in applying policy which will provide meaningful financial reports. If a standard does not exist for a specific transaction, preparers are told to look for alternative GAAP reporting requirements. Any GAAP with a comparable Conceptual Framework to IFRS will be allowed. Under this system, managerial manipulation would seem inevitable. The possibilities exist that entities in Canada, adopting IFRS in 2011, will encounter situations where IFRS does not offer guidance. In this circumstance, managers will be allowed to shop for guidance from GAAP alternatives, as long as these alternatives result from a conceptual framework comparable to IFRS.

The SEC has provided added incentive for the convergence of US GAAP and IFRS by allowing entities reporting under full IFRS to avoid costly 20-F reconciliations. Note that the SEC requires application of full IFRS, which does not allow carve-outs. In order to comply with this provision of SEC reporting, entities must be in compliance with IFRS as written, not as nationally revised. The following section provides a technical analysis of the current differences in US GAAP and IFRS and provides discussion concerning the potential carve-outs of convergence and their transparency effects.

Part Three

Technical Analysis: US GAAP versus IFRS

Subsequent sections provide a concise comparison of the technical differences between US GAAP and IFRS. Such differences may lead to differences in transparency. The analysis begins with an overview of differences in presentation, progresses through technical differences of specific transactions and concludes with transition issues that should be expected when (or if) the US converts to IFRS.

5. Presentation of Financial Information

Both US GAAP and IFRS require entities to present a balance sheet, an income statement, a statement of changes in equity, a cash flow statement and explanatory notes that provide additional disclosure to users. Both require comparative information, and US entities also must comply with additional SEC filing requirements. Entities claiming to report under the guidance of IFRS are required to provide an explicit declaration of compliance with all provisions of IFRS (e. g. no carve-outs). IFRS explicitly defines the presentation requirements of the financial statements.

Presentation has been shown to affect perceptions of financial reporting. For example, in 2000, accounting researchers noted:

> Statement of Financial Accounting Standards (SFAS) No. 130 requires companies to report comprehensive income in a primary financial statement, but allows its presentation in either a statement of comprehensive income or a statement of stockholders' equity (Financial Accounting Standards Board [FASB] 1997). In an experiment, we examine whether and how alternative presentation formats affect nonprofessional investors' processing of comprehensive-income information, specifically, information disclosing the volatility of unrealized

gains on available-for-sale marketable securities. The results show that nonprofessional investors' judgments of corporate and management performance reflect the volatility of comprehensive income only when it is presented in a statement of comprehensive income.[22]

Similar behavioural tendencies have been noted for professional investors, professional financial analysts and other users of financial reports.[23] Presentation affects transparency and influences perceptions of quality. As convergence continues, presentation of financial information is still a matter for discussion between IASB and FASB.

A. Balance sheet items

Under the guidance of IAS 1, *Presentation of Financial Statements*, entities are required to present a statement of financial position that includes, at a minimum, the following items: PP&E, biological assets, intangible assets, financial assets, tax assets split into current and non-current portions, assets held for sale, associates reported under the equity method, investment property, inventories, trade and other receivables, and cash. Note that under IFRS, the order of presentation may be reversed from the most-to-least liquid listing preferred under

---

[22] L. Maines and L. McDaniel, "Effects of Comprehensive-Income Characteristics on Nonprofessional Investors' Judgments: The Role of Financial-Statement Presentation Format" *Accounting Review*, 75:2 (2000), pp. 179–207.

[23] Also see: D. E. Hirst and P. E. Hopkins, "Comprehensive income reporting and analysts' valuation judgments", *Journal of Accounting Research* 36, Supplement (1998), pp. 47–75, P. E. Hopkins, "The effect of financial statement classification of hybrid financial instruments on financial analysts' stock price judgments", *Journal of Accounting Research* 34, Supplement (1996), pp. 33–50, J. E. Hunton and R. A. McEwen "An assessment of the relation between analysts' earnings forecast accuracy, motivational incentives, and cognitive information search strategy", *The Accounting Review* 72 (1997), pp. 497–516, E. E. Comiskey, R. A. McEwen and C. Mulford, "A Test of Pro Forma Consolidation of Finance Subsidiaries", *Financial Management* 24 (1987), pp. 45-50.

US GAAP. IFRS also requires explicit reporting of trade and other payables, tax liabilities split into current and non-current portions, provisions, financial liabilities, liabilities held for sale, non-controlling interests, capital accounts and reserves. Provisions, as defined under IFRS, are not allowed on US GAAP balance sheets, but similar liabilities, called contingencies, are required under US GAAP. In more expansive terms, IAS 1 requires:[24]

(a) property, plant and equipment;

(b) investment property;

(c) intangible assets;

(d) financial assets (excluding amounts shown under e, h and i);

(e) investments accounted for using the equity method;

(f) biological assets;

(g) inventories;

(h) trade and other receivables;

(i) cash and cash equivalents;

(j) the total of assets classified as held for sale and assets included in disposal groups classified as held for sale in accordance with IFRS 5 *Non-current Assets Held for Sale and Discontinued Operations*;

(k) trade and other payables;

(l) provisions;

(m) financial liabilities (excluding amounts shown under k and l);

(n) liabilities and assets for current tax, as defined in IAS 12 *Income Taxes*;

---

[24] IAS 1, *Presentation of Financial Statements*, paragraph 54.

(o) deferred tax liabilities and deferred tax assets, as defined in IAS 12;

(p) liabilities included in disposal groups classified as held for sale in accordance with IFRS 5;

(q) non-controlling interests, presented within equity;

(r) issued capital and reserves attributable to owners of the parent.

Interestingly, US GAAP allows (although strongly discourages) use of what is called the mezzanine section of the balance sheet. The mezzanine falls between liabilities and equity. Currently, non-controlling interests, some deferred tax liabilities and other problematic debt/equity items are posted in this section of the balance sheet. Under convergence, non-controlling interests (called Minority Interests prior to FAS 160) and mandatorily redeemable preferred stock will no longer be allowed to be presented in this area.

B. Income statement items

Presentation for the income statement differs somewhat between US GAAP and IFRS. IFRS does not really prescribe a format, although expenses are required to be stated by function or by nature, whereas under US GAAP, expenses are stated by function. Expenses stated by function focus on the nature of the activity the expense relates to (i.e. production, distribution, selling or administrative) while expenses stated by nature focus on the type of expense itself (i.e. salaries, taxes or depreciation). Under both US GAAP and IFRS, income attributable to non-controlling interests is required to be separately disclosed.

Extraordinary items

One major difference between US GAAP and IFRS is the prohibition against reporting a line item called Extraordinary Items for IFRS, but its continued use under US GAAP reporting. Extraordinary Items are deemed to be both unusual and infrequent (APB 30, Codification Glossary and Codification 225-20) and must be classified as such in relation to the environment in which an entity operates. In certain circumstances, items which are clearly extraordinary may be precluded from this classification (e.g. losses under US GAAP from events related to September 11, 2001). In a similar manner, FASB has deemed items which may be both usual and frequent to be classified as extraordinary although these items clearly violate the rules for reporting Extraordinary Items. For example, until recently, FASB mandated that gains and losses from debt repurchases must be classified as Extraordinary Items.

Due to these seemingly arbitrary classification schemes, elimination of Extraordinary Items as an income statement item may seem to enhance transparency and the predictability of income. As was originally intended, non-recurring gains and losses included in ordinary income could serve to diminish the predictability of earnings since, by definition, they were not expected to occur again. By designating these items as extraordinary and forcing separate disclosure on the income statement, the intent of APB 30 was to enhance the predictive nature of the earnings measure. Numerous abuses of the rule may have caused the opposite effect. Through managerial misdirection and complicit auditors, items which should have been classified as extraordinary gains were included with ordinary income, while items which should have been classified as ordinary losses were afforded extraordinary status. In either of these latter settings, transparency and quality were diminished.

C. Comprehensive income, earnings and earnings per share

IAS 1, as amended in 2008[25], allows an entity to present a single statement of comprehensive income, or two statements displaying income components and other comprehensive income components. Under IAS 1[26], the information required to be presented in the statement of comprehensive income includes, at a minimum:

(a) revenue;

(b) finance costs;

(c) share of the profit or loss of associates and joint ventures accounted for using the equity method;

(d) tax expense;

(e) a single amount comprising the total of:

　(1) the post-tax profit or loss of discontinued operations;

　(2) the post-tax gain or loss recognized on the measurement to fair value, less costs to sell, or on the disposal of the assets or disposal group(s) constituting the discontinued operation;

(h) profit or loss;

(i) each component of other comprehensive income classified by nature (excluding amounts in h);

(j) share of the other comprehensive income of associates and joint ventures accounted for using the equity method;

　(1) total comprehensive income.[27]

---

[25] eifrs.iasb.org/eifrs/stdcontent/2008_Bound_Volume/IAS1o_2007-09-06_en-3.html#F3903008 paragraph 81.

[26] See paragraph 82.

[27] Id., paragraph 82.

Profit and loss items and comprehensive income items include those attributable to non-controlling interests (minority interests) and owners of the parent entity. Entities are required to present subheadings for all statements if the presentation is relevant to understanding the financial report[28]. Other comprehensive income includes items of income and expense, including *reclassification adjustments*, which are not recognized in profit or loss as required or permitted by other IFRSs. Such items include:

(a) changes in revaluation surplus (see IAS 16 *Property, Plant and Equipment* and IAS 38 *Intangible Assets*);

(b) actuarial gains and losses on defined benefit plans recognized in accordance with paragraph 93A of IAS 19 *Employee Benefits*;

(c) gains and losses arising from translating the *financial statements* of a foreign operation (see IAS 21 *The Effects of Changes in Foreign Exchange Rates*);

(d) gains and losses on remeasuring available-for-sale financial assets (see IAS 39 *Financial Instruments: Recognition and Measurement*);

(e) the effective portion of gains and losses on hedging instruments in a cash flow hedge (see IAS 39).[29]

An entity may present components of *other comprehensive income* either net of related tax effects or before related tax effects with one amount shown for the aggregate amount of income tax relating to those components.[30]

---

[28] Id., paragraph 83.

[29] Id., paragraph 7.

[30] IAS 1, paragraph 90.

Items will flow from the other comprehensive income section to the income section. For example, assume unrealized gains and losses from available-for-sale securities are recognized into other comprehensive income in 20X0. At sale, in 20X1, gains and losses will be realized. Such gains must be removed from other comprehensive income, as reflected in 20X0, and a reclassification adjustment must be included in other comprehensive income to identify the realization of an unrealized holding gain or loss. Failure to remove the components from other comprehensive income would result in double counting since realized gains or losses will also be reported in income.

IAS 33, *Earnings per Share*, provides guidance related to EPS presentation on the statement of comprehensive income. Paragraphs 4 and 4A establish:

> When an entity presents both consolidated financial statements and separate financial statements prepared in accordance with IAS 27 Consolidated and Separate Financial Statements, the disclosures required by this Standard need be presented only on the basis of the consolidated information. An entity that chooses to disclose earnings per share based on its separate financial statements shall present such earnings per share information only in its statement of comprehensive income. An entity shall not present such earnings per share information in the consolidated financial statements[31].

Paragraph 4A requires that entities presenting components of profit or loss in a separate income statement (as allowed by AIS 1, paragraph 81) present EPS only in that statement[32].

---

[31] IAS 33, paragraph 4.

[32] Id., paragraph 4A.

IAS 33 emphasizes guidance related to the denominator of the earnings per share measure. Recognizing that numerous accounting alternatives will affect the numerator of this measure, the IASB presents guidance focusing on how to measure the denominator of earnings per share. IAS 33 and FASB 128 were written and revised to ensure convergence and currently contain few discrepancies in the calculation of the denominator. IFRS also requires presentation of a statement of changes in equity which separates total comprehensive income into the amounts attributable to owners, and amounts attributable to non-controlling interests. IFRS requires extensive reconciliation of beginning to ending amounts for each equity component including changes resulting from profit and loss, each item of comprehensive income and transactions with owners.[33] Thus, IFRS guidance enforces no conceptual distinction between flows derived from earnings and those derived from equity sources. This notion tends to converge on the US GAAP definition of comprehensive income.

Under US GAAP, revenues are recognized when realized, or when realizable and earned. While the concepts of recognition and realization are generally understood, the concept of earned revenue requires additional discussion. Both FASB and the SEC provide guidance. Specifically, FASB considers revenue to be earned when the seller has substantially accomplished what it must do to be entitled to the benefits represented by the revenues.[34]

---

[33] IAS 1, paragraph 106.

[34] CON 5, ¶ 83.

The SEC defines four criteria for earning revenue:

1   persuasive evidence of an arrangement exists;

2   delivery has occurred or services have been rendered;

3   the seller's price to the buyer is fixed or determinable; and

4   collectability is reasonably assured.[35]

Under both definitions, the accrual basis of accounting requires revenues to be recognized when earned, rather than only at the cash exchange point.

Revenues directly affect performance measures. Under current US GAAP, there are three general measures of firm performance required to be reported in an entity's financial statements: earnings, earnings per share and comprehensive income. FASB's Concept Statement No. 5 describes earnings similarly to what is currently referred to as net income in practice.[36] Generally, earnings will include all accrual-based revenue or gain items less any accrual-based expense or loss items. Thus, revenues, defined as inflows resulting from an entity's ongoing operations, and gains, defined as inflows from incidental transactions, will directly increase earnings. Similarly, expenses (outflows from ongoing operations) and losses (outflows from incidental transactions) directly reduce these measures of entity performance. The concept of earnings, as opposed to the concept of income, is associated with items that are period specific and are related to the degree of cash-to-cash completion. Thus, earnings are focused on operations and ancillary activities that will be substantially completed during the reporting period.

---

[35] SEC Staff Accounting Bulletin No. 104, Revenue Recognition Corrected Copy (December 2003) [hereinafter SAB 104] page 2.

[36] CON 5, par 34.

The metric earnings per share expresses earnings available to common shareholders relative to a measure of the number of shares they hold. While the concept seems relatively straightforward, its application is not. Measurement issues associated with income, shares held (issued and outstanding and not repurchased by the corporation), and securities that potentially may be held introduce complexity into calculation of this performance measure.

Items affecting earnings and earnings per share also affect the final measure of entity performance required by US GAAP. Comprehensive income includes all inflows and outflows that affect an entity except those that result from investments from, or distributions to, owners. CON 5 suggests that the difference between earnings and comprehensive income is not well understood, but the distinction is important in external financial reporting.

Statement of Financial Accounting Standards No. 130 (FAS 130), *Reporting Comprehensive Income*[37] (codification Topic 220), does not completely specify when to measure, how to recognize or what to include in comprehensive income. However, general practice has included items such as the effects of valuation adjustments applied to non-current marketable equity securities, pension gains and losses, and also some foreign currency adjustments. Thus, all items included in earnings are also included in comprehensive income, but the reverse is not true. Items exist, such as valuation adjustments applied to non-current equity, that are not specific to the period. These items are included in comprehensive income but are excluded from earnings.

---

[37] Financial Accounting Standards Board, Statement of Financial Accounting Standards No. 130, *Reporting Comprehensive Income* (June 1997) [hereinafter FAS 130].

Neither current earnings nor EPS provides a user with consistently transparent and high-quality information for making predictions about entity performance. Instead, accounting researchers suggest we should focus an income measure that corresponds to the amount that can be paid out as dividends while leaving an entity equally well-off at the beginning and end of a period, which is approximated by comprehensive income. Transparent financial statements should openly and clearly reflect change in this key measure of performance.

D. Statement of cash flows

The statement of cash flows serves much the same purpose and follows similar guidance for both IFRS and US GAAP reporting. Entities report the change in cash across the period, and summarize cash inflows/outflows into operating, investing or financing components. Operating cash flows are important in financial analysis, and are defined by omission. That is, financing cash flows arise from transactions relating to equity and debt, and investing cash flows relate to non-current assets. All other cash flows are considered to be operating.

A major classification difference between IFRS and US GAAP resides in the operating section of the statement of cash flows. For US GAAP, interest paid or received is an operating item. This controversial position was taken when FAS 95 was adopted in 1987. While many respondents favored classifying interest paid as a cash outflow for financing activities, and interest and dividends received as cash inflows from investing activities, the board took the position that cash flows from operating activities should reflect the cash effects of transactions and other events that enter into the determination of net income. Opponents of this view suggested that interest paid, like dividends paid, is a direct consequence of a financing decision and should be classified as a cash outflow for financing activities.[38] Interest is considered to be outside of operations in the US GAAP income statement. IFRS allows interest paid to be classified as financing or operating, and interest received to be investing or operating.

E. Interim and segment reporting

Fundamental reporting differences arise between US GAAP and IFRS in the approaches used to report results for interim periods. US GAAP considers each interim period as integral to the full year. Thus, US GAAP requires allocations of costs among periods. IFRS considers each interim period as a discrete reporting period. Under this treatment, entities must apply the same principles as they would for year-end. The US GAAP integral method can result in diminished earnings quality to the extent that users form expectations about annual earnings from interim earnings numbers. Under the integral method, the annual earnings per share measure will not necessarily be the sum of the four quarterly earnings measures. Segment reporting guidance under US GAAP is converging toward IFRS and no carve-outs have been identified. Under IFRS, entities must use the same policies for segment reporting that they use to prepare their consolidated financial statements.

F. Assets held for sale and discontinued operations

Under IFRS, assets held for sale must meet restrictive conditions to be classified as such. First, they must be available for immediate sale, and the sale must be highly probable. Under this condition, management

---

[38] FAS 95, par 87 and 88. There is no codification number for basis language since it is not considered to be authoritative.

must have an active plan to sell the assets at a reasonable price. To be classified as held for sale, the sales plan must not be significantly changed and should occur within one year. As with other assets, those held for sale must be tested for impairment; however, these assets are not depreciated. Discontinued operations are those which have been held for sale, or sold during the reporting period.

Presentation differences between US GAAP and IFRS are noted in the definition of a discontinued operation. Under US GAAP, reporting a discontinued operation is less restrictive, and disposals are more likely to qualify as discontinued operations. IFRS maintains a more restrictive principle that discontinued operations can be clearly distinguished from the entity, and that asset groups that do not meet this requirement are precluded from being designated as discontinued operations. Convergence is expected on this issue.

G. Capital

IFRS risk assessment includes specific disclosure about capital from an entity. IAS 1 requires disclosure of the following:

(a) qualitative information about the entity's objectives, policies and processes for managing capital, including:

    (1) a description of what it manages as capital;

    (2) when an entity is subject to externally imposed capital requirements, the nature of those requirements and how those requirements are incorporated into the management of capital; and

    (3) how it is meeting its objectives for managing capital.

(b) summary quantitative data about what it manages as capital. Some entities regard some financial liabilities (e.g. some forms of subordinated debt) as part of capital. Other entities regard capital as excluding some components of equity (e.g. components arising from cash flow hedges).

(c) any changes in (a) and (b) from the previous period.

(d) whether, during the period, it complied with any externally imposed capital requirements to which it is subject.

(e) when the entity has not complied with such externally imposed capital requirements, the consequences of such non-compliance.[39]

Entities also must provide disclosure of:

(a) the amount of dividends proposed or declared before the *financial statements* were authorized for issue but not recognized as a distribution to *owners* during the period, and the related amount per share; and

(b) the amount of any cumulative preference dividends not recognized.[40]

H. Stockholders' equity

Accounting Research Bulletin No. 43 (ARB 43, Codification sections 505 Equity) provides general guidance for US GAAP in presentation of Stockholder's Equity. In general, guidance is limited to treatment of warrants with convertible instruments, redeemable preferred stock,

---

[39] IAS 1, paragraph 135.

[40] IAS 1, paragraph 137.

stock dividends and splits, treasury stock and share-based payments to non-employees. IAS 32 presents guidance for IFRS. Few differences remain between US GAAP and IFRS in presentation of stockholder's equity.

I. Notes

IFRS requires extensive disclosure not required under US GAAP. IAS 1, paragraph 112 requires that entities shall:

(a) present information about the basis of preparation of the financial statements and the specific accounting policies used in accordance with [IAS] paragraphs 117-124;

(b) disclose the information required by IFRSs that is not presented elsewhere in the financial statements; and

(c) provide information that is not presented elsewhere in the financial statements, but is relevant to an understanding of any of them.[41]

Notes must be presented in a systematic manner, and are required to help the user understand financial presentation. They must be cross-referenced to each item in the financial statements. Presentation order is prescribed by IAS 1, paragraph 114.

An entity normally presents notes in the following order, to assist users in understanding the financial statements and to compare them with financial statements of other entities:

(a) statement of compliance with IFRSs;

(b) summary of significant accounting policies applied;

---

[41] Id., paragraph 112.

(c) supporting information for items presented in the statements of financial position and of comprehensive income, in the separate income statement (if presented), and in the statements of changes in equity and of cash flows, in the order in which each statement and each line item is presented; and

(d) other disclosures, including:

(A) contingent liabilities and unrecognized contractual commitments, and

(B) non-financial disclosures, e.g. the entity's financial risk management objectives and policies.[42]

Entities are required to present detailed analyses of significant accounting policies, including the basis of measurement used for financial reporting. Carve-outs are required to be identified. If measurement assumptions have been used, then entities are required to disclose adequate information for an informed user to be able to understand the transaction. Sources of uncertainty associated with estimates and managerial judgment which may have a material adjustment within the next year must be disclosed. Fair value estimates based on market prices are not required uncertainty disclosures, but estimates based on inputs, other than those at level one, require extensive disclosure.

The extensive disclosure requirements of IFRS may enhance transparency, yet still seem troubling when viewed in the context of US markets and ongoing managerial misstatements concerning financial reports. Entities may provide extensive disclosure, but even with audited statements, deliberate misstatement can occur.

---

[42] Id., paragraph 114.

6. Related Party Transactions

Related party transactions occur when an entity engages in financial activities that do not meet the arm's-length assumption. Such transactions require mandatory disclosure. Entities are required under US GAAP and IFRS to disclose transfer of resources, services or obligations to counterparties that are controlled by the entity, have significant interest in the entity or joint control over the entity. Indicators of influence include transactions at non-market rates, sharing of resources, engagement in significant transactions and the presence of common members of the board. Management and family members of management also are considered to be related parties.

IFRS exempts some types of transactions from these disclosure requirements. For example, entities that are related only because one party is controlled or significantly influenced by a state and the counterparty is also controlled or significantly influenced by a state – with there being no other indicators of control – are excluded from disclosing transactions between the parties. Transactions with the state are required to be disclosed.

7. Subsequent Events

Both US GAAP and IFRS require recognition of events occurring after the reporting period under certain circumstances. These events occur between the end of the fiscal year and the date of authorization (IFRS) or the date of publication (US GAAP) of the financial statements. They can result in gains or losses and their recognition and/or disclosure depends on whether they arose from conditions that existed at the end of the period, or conditions that occurred after the period.

Events that arose from conditions in existence at the end of the period are adjusting events and are recognized, under IFRS, if they occur prior to the statements being authorized. Since authorization of financial statements may depend on board approval or other internal actions, judgment is required in the determination of whether or not to recognize the event rather than merely disclose it. IFRS requires extensive disclosure of authorization, adjusting events and non-adjusting events. US GAAP and IFRS are expected to converge on this issue.

8. Revenue Recognition

In December 2003, the SEC published SAB 104, which supersedes portions of other SEC guidance on revenue recognition.[43] The statement, in conjunction with FASB's Concepts Statement 5 (CON 5), provides general US GAAP in the area of revenue recognition. More specific industry guidance is provided by FAS 45, *Accounting for Franchise Fee Revenue*; FAS 48, *Revenue Recognition When Right of Return Exists*; FAS 66, *Accounting for Sales of Real Estate*; and a series of SOPs and EITFs. All authoritative guidance pertaining to revenue recognition is provided in FASB's codification under topic No. 605, Revenue Recognition.

The term "revenue" relates to inflows from an entity's central ongoing operations, those activities that produce goods or render services. Revenue is recognized (taken through the accounting process) when it is realized (cash has been exchanged) or realizable (an account

---

[43] SEC Staff Accounting Bulletin: No. 104, Topic 13: Revenue Recognition (December 2003).

receivable has been established) and earned. Under US GAAP, revenues are earned when the entity has substantially completed what it must accomplish to be entitled to the benefits of the revenues.[44] The SEC staff has set specific criteria for revenue recognition and maintains the position that revenues have been earned if all of the following criteria have been met:

(a) Persuasive evidence of an arrangement exists. The SEC suggests that the use of the term "arrangement" is meant to identify a final understanding between the buyer and the seller as to the specific nature and terms of the transaction. Revenue recognition under IFRS (as provided in IAS 18) does not have similar criteria.

(b) Delivery has occurred or services have been rendered. This criterion provides the SEC's view on what an entity must accomplish to be entitled to the benefits of the revenues. It infers that, for products, title must pass before revenues can be recognized. Similarly, IAS 18 indicates that a sale has occurred when the risks and rewards of ownership have been transferred. Under IAS 18, the seller can have no continuing involvement or control.

(c) The seller's price to the buyer is fixed or determinable. Price determination is central to a sales transaction. Under US GAAP, sales with a high degree of refund or adjustment may not meet this criterion. IFRS requires only that the sales amount can be reliably measured.

---

[44] CON 5, ¶83b.

(d) Collectability is reasonably assured. In the event that cash exchange will follow the merchandise or service exchange, the collection of cash must be reasonably assured in order for revenue to be recognized under US GAAP.[45] IAS 18 requirements differ slightly in that in order for revenue to be recognized, it is probable that benefits will flow to the seller.

Each of the criteria provides an area of concern for transparency and quality. For example, the requirement that 'persuasive evidence of an arrangement exists' may depend on an entity's customary business practices or on industry practices. Entities that ordinarily require written sales agreements may be precluded from recognizing revenues on oral sales agreements, especially if administrative approval from the buyer is required.[46] Entities may use other types of agreements such as online ordering or confirmed purchase orders. These practices are evidence that an arrangement exists and revenues are recognized when the appropriate order has been placed. Arrangements such as cancellation, termination or other provisions that negate the sale could be an indicator that revenue recognition is not appropriate.[47] However, prevailing practice is defined by management and is thus subject to manipulation.

SAB 104 provides guidance related to consignment arrangements and states that these transactions are not considered to be revenues until the title passes to the ultimate buyer.

---

[45] SAB 104, p. 10.

[46] SAB 104, p. 13.

[47] SAB 104, p. 14.

Transactions similar to consignment sales preclude revenue recognition, even if title has passed to the buyer, if any of the following exist:

(a) The buyer has the right to return the product and the buyer does not pay at the time of sale and is not obligated to pay at a specified date or dates.

(b) The buyer has the right to return the product and the buyer's obligation to pay is based on a resell of the product.

The buyer has the right to return the product and the seller would forgive the obligation in the event of theft or physical destruction of the product.

The buyer has the right to return the product and the buyer does not have economic substance apart from the seller. In this setting, the seller is prohibited from earning revenues by selling products to itself.

The buyer has the right to return the product and the seller must perform significant actions to resell the product for the buyer.[48]

In each of these situations, revenue recognition would be inappropriate since the revenues have not been earned. The ability of the buyer to return the product in conjunction with a non-cash sale and, in some cases, failure to establish a valid account receivable precludes revenue recognition. Revenue recognition is also precluded if:

(a) The seller is required to repurchase the product at a price that substantially covers all costs incurred by the buyer. Indicators of this condition include situations where the seller provides interest-free or below market financing until the product is resold, or the seller pays interest on behalf of the buyer, or the seller refunds interest expense on financing once the product has been resold.

---

[48] SAB 104, p. 14.

(b) The product is delivered for demonstration purposes.[49]

In each of these instances, the seller is financing a transaction with substantial responsibilities until the resale of the product, or the transaction is not intended to be a valid sale. Notice that these transactions introduce a high degree of uncertainty into issues of revenue recognition. The SEC suggests that these and many other types of consignment and financing require managerial judgment in determining whether to recognize revenues.[50] SAB 104 does allow revenue recognition for sellers who enter into arrangements with entities in countries where title cannot pass until payment has been made. If all other revenue recognition criteria have been met, the SEC suggests revenue recognition with a valid account receivable is permissible.

A. Bill-and-hold sales

Problems also exist in determining when title has passed to the buyer. In the past, entities recognized revenues on bill-and-hold orders. For example, if a buyer purchases products from a seller, but the buyer does not wish to take delivery until a later period, then the seller may question whether they have met criteria for revenue recognition. The SEC suggests that the seller is not entitled to recognize revenues until title has passed to the buyer. Passage of title can depend on shipping agreements, but generally title passes when a product is delivered to the buyer if the terms are FOB destination, and title passes when the product has been delivered to the common carrier if the terms are FOB shipping point.[51]

---

[49] SAB 104, p. 17.

[50] SAB 104, p. 18.

[51] SAB 104, p. 20.

Entities are allowed to recognize revenues on bill-and-hold sales before delivery of goods, but only if title has passed. The SEC allows the seller to recognize revenues in these transactions when:

(a) Risks of ownership have passed to the buyer.

(b) The buyer has made a fixed commitment to purchase the goods and, preferably, the agreement is in writing.

(c) The buyer, and not the seller, asks for the bill-and-hold arrangement. The request should be in writing and the buyer must have a substantive business purpose for asking for the bill-and-hold arrangement.

(d) There must be a fixed schedule for delivery.

(e) There are no further performance obligations required of the seller.

(f) The goods have been segregated from the seller's inventory and are not available for sales to others.

(g) The product is ready for shipment.

Bill-and-hold transactions provide the opportunity for the seller to manage earnings by shifting the revenue recognition timing from later to earlier periods. SAB 104 provides guidance to financial statement preparers in determining if the transaction is one of substance over form. Specifically, preparers are cautioned to consider the payment date and whether the seller has modified this date in the past for the buyer or other types of agreements that introduce uncertainty into the transaction.[52]

---

[52] SAB 104, pp. 22-23.

Sellers also are precluded from recognizing revenues from transactions if uncertainty exists about the buyer's acceptance of the product. If substantive testing and modifications are part of the sales agreement, revenue recognition is not warranted. If the arrangement allows the buyer to accept the product and then return it after a trial period, revenue recognition may not be permissible. Most sales have some provision for return of a product if the buyer is dissatisfied. If the transaction is solely for evaluation purposes, then revenue cannot be recognized. If the transaction is a sale with the right of return, then revenue recognition is permissible as long as the seller also estimates the amount of future returns.[53]

B. Long-term construction contracts

Other problems that arise in revenue recognition include those associated with long-term construction or contracting. In these situations, an extended period is necessary to complete the product or provide a service. Entities are required to recognize revenues across the life of the project using the percentage-of-completion method, unless they can not dependably estimate the costs and time to complete the contract. In such a setting, entities recognize all revenues at the completion of the contract. Transparency and quality are affected by judgment; aggressive estimates shift revenues into earlier periods while underestimates of progress allow revenues to be shifted to later periods.

---

[53] Financial Accounting Standards Board, Statement of Financial Accounting Standards No. 48, *Revenue Recognition When Right of Return Exists* (June 1981), ¶ 6.

C. Software

Software presents problems for preparers in revenue recognition. Revenue on software that requires no additional enhancements or upgrades is recognized in a manner similar to other items: when evidence of an arrangement exists, delivery has occurred, the price has been fixed and collectibility is probable. Revenue on software with multiple license arrangements for upgrades, enhancements or significant customer support services is required to be allocated to the various parts of the agreement based on vendor-specific objective estimates (VSOE) of relative fair values.

D. Multiple deliverables

Multiple deliverables follow much the same type of guidance. In general, if one deliverable of a series of multiple deliverables has value to the customer and reliable evidence of fair value exists, the seller allocates revenues to the separate units based on their relative fair values. If fair value exists for items to be delivered in the future, but not for items already delivered, then revenue is allocated to the delivered items computed as the remainder of revenue after removing the fair value of the yet to be delivered items. The calculation of fair value under this circumstance is highly dependent on managerial judgment and the resultant earnings may be of diminished quality. Note that customer loyalty programs may also be accounted for under an incremental cost method that allocates costs instead of allocating revenue based on fair value.

E. Disclosure

US GAAP requires that entities should disclose information about the important judgments regarding accounting principles used to recognize revenues. In general, the disclosure should encompass important judgments as to appropriateness of principles relating to recognition of revenue and allocation of asset costs to current and future periods; in particular, it should encompass those accounting principles and methods that involve any of the following:

(a) a selection from existing acceptable alternatives;

(b) principles and methods peculiar to the industry in which the reporting entity operates, even if such principles and methods are predominantly followed in that industry;

(c) unusual or innovative applications of generally accepted accounting principles (and, as applicable, of principles and methods peculiar to the industry in which the reporting entity operates).[54]

Revenue recognition under any method other than cash exchange transactions with delivery at point of sale requires some degree of judgment. Since numerous business transactions are not cash at delivery, the SEC believes that revenue recognition policies are always relevant to users and suggests disclosure of such policies is always appropriate.[55] Disclosure may be provided through many avenues, including Management's Discussion and Analysis of Results (MD&A).

---

[54] American Institute of Certified Public Accountants, Accounting Principles Board Opinion 22, Disclosure of Accounting Policies (April 1972) ¶ 12.

[55] SAB 104, p. 75.

MD&A is designed to provide users with both historical and prospective analyses of financial condition, with an emphasis on information that would be useful in predicting the future financial condition of the entity. In terms of revenue transactions, the SEC suggests the following are appropriate for disclosure in the MD&A section:

(a) End of period shipments that significantly reduce customer backlogs but that will also result in lower shipments in the future.

(b) Granting extended payment terms that will result in longer collection and slower cash inflows from operations, and the effect on liquidity and capital resources.

(d) Changing trends in shipments that could reasonably be expected to affect future sales or returns.

(e) Increasing sales of products with smaller or larger profit margins.

(f) Seasonality in sales.

(h) Gains and losses from sales of assets other than inventory.[56]

Unlike the numerous pronouncements on revenue recognition provided in US GAAP, recognition under IFRS is summarized only by IAS 18, *Revenue*, IAS 11, *Construction Contracts* and three interpretations. In general, revenue recognition under the provisions of IFRS focus on the probability that the seller will benefit, and that revenue can be measured. Under the provisions of IAS 18, revenue may not be recognized if the seller has additional obligations not covered by normal warranty provisions. If the sale is contingent on the resale of the product, or if the sale is contingent upon significant installation

---

[56] SAB 104, p. 77.

procedures which have not been completed, then revenue may not be recognized. Under both US GAAP and IFRS, if the buyer can rescind the purchase or can influence the price, revenue is not recognized.

F. Differences in revenue recognition

Fundamental differences exist between US GAAP and IFRS in recognizing revenues. Both methods require revenue to be recognized at fair value, but IFRS allows a discounted present value to represent fair value in many more situations than US GAAP. Fair value reporting affects revenue measurement, especially in situations where one transaction contains multiple deliverables. For example, under IFRS, loyalty programs (awards for product use) are treated like multiple deliverable transactions, and some of the proceeds of the initial sale are recognized as a liability. The liability is measured at the amount the award could have been sold for separately, and both revenue and the liability are recognized at fair value. Under the provisions of IFRIC 13, the deferred revenue is recognized only when the seller has provided the award, or has paid a third party to do so. US GAAP accounts for such awards as contingencies. Note that under IFRS, the sales price is allocated on relative fair values, but fair value may be computed as the present value of estimated cash inflows for each stage. Transparency and quality may be diminished if present value is not a good approximation of fair value.

Construction accounting also offers a difference between US GAAP and IFRS. Under both US GAAP and IFRS, percentage of completion is required unless estimates are not dependable. Under US GAAP, if estimates required under the percentage of completions method are not dependable, then preparers use the completed contract method which recognizes revenues only when the contract is substantially complete. Under IFRS, completed contract accounting is not allowed. Instead, if estimates are not reliable, then revenues are recognized only for contract costs that will probably be recovered, and all contract costs are expensed as incurred. Under such a system, profits may be accelerated into earlier periods.

Under IFRS, software revenue is recognized under a percentage of completion type system which includes after delivery enhancements and customer support. Vendor-specific objective estimates (VSOE) are not required. Thus, service-type contracts as well as construction contracts recognize revenues using percentage of completion under IFRS, a system prohibited by US GAAP for contracts other than construction contracts.

Under IFRS revenue recognition is more transparent. Revenues are recognized only when the risks and rewards of ownership have been transferred, the purchaser has obtained control of the goods, the revenues can be measured reliably and it is probable (there is at least a 50% probability) that the seller will obtain economic benefits. Note IFRS holds a higher standard for revenue recognition, requiring that both risk and rewards of ownership have passed to the purchaser. FASB and IASB are currently working to present a unified definition of revenue which will be reflected in IFRS.

Transactions producing revenues will also produce an expense and expenses are matched to the revenues that produced them. For example, sales of goods will produce revenues and will also produce an expense (e.g. cost of goods sold) related to the asset given up in the sale. Expenses that cannot be explicitly linked to revenues, such as the cost of a long-term asset, are systematically and rationally allocated against revenues (depreciated or amortized). In general, revenues plus gains, less expenses and losses, defines earnings. Earnings available to common shareholders (i.e. net of preferred shareholder dividends) expressed relative to the shares held by the common shareholders form the basis of earnings per share.

Revenue shifting, questionable customer acceptance practices, bill-and-hold sales, and poor disclosure along with the inexact nature of revenue recognition, provide numerous avenues for diminished earnings quality and transparency under both US GAAP and IFRS. The quality of revenues derived under fair value reporting is questionable, especially in circumstances where multiple deliverables comprise the contract and identical or similar values for all parts of the contract do not exist. In such settings, revenue can be shifted from period to period based on managerial judgment. Revenue recognition convergence is highly desirable and is currently under discussion by a joint committee that anticipates convergence by 2011.

9. Assets

Assets are characterized as having a probable future benefit. A particular entity can obtain the benefit and control others' access to it, and the transaction or other event giving rise to the entity's right to, or control of, the benefit has already occurred.[57] Assets represent probable future economic benefits and current assets are those expected to be converted to cash within one year, or the operating cycle, whichever is longer.[58]

---

[57] CON 6, ¶26.

[58] ARB 43, Ch. 3A, ¶5 (Codification 210-10).

Under IFRS, entities are required to classify an asset as current when:

(a) it expects to realize the asset, or intends to sell or consume it, in its normal operating cycle;

(b) it holds the asset primarily for the purpose of trading;

(c) it expects to realize the asset within 12 months after the reporting period; or

(d) the asset is cash or a cash equivalent (as defined in IAS 7) unless the asset is restricted from being exchanged or used to settle a liability for at least 12 months after the reporting period.[59]

All other assets are considered to be non-current.

Current liabilities are defined as those where:

(a) an entity expects to settle the liability in its normal operating cycle;

(b) an entity holds the liability primarily for the purpose of trading;

(c) the liability is due to be settled within 12 months after the reporting period; or

(d) the entity does not have an unconditional right to defer settlement of the liability for at least 12 months after the reporting period.[60]

All other liabilities are non-current.

IFRS requires, at a minimum, explicit listing of PP&E, biological assets, intangible assets, financial assets, tax assets split into current and non-current portions, assets held for sale, associates reported under the equity method, investment property, inventories, trade and other

---

[59] IAS 1, paragraph 66.

[60] IAS 1, paragraph 69.

receivables, and cash. Other assets may be listed if appropriate. With the exception of inventory accounting, IFRS treatment of current assets is not significantly different from US GAAP treatment. Non-current assets differ significantly.

A. Inventory

The term *inventory* identifies goods awaiting sale (the merchandise of a trading concern and the finished goods of a manufacturer), goods in the course of production (work in process), and goods to be consumed directly or indirectly in production (raw materials and supplies).[61] Under US GAAP, inventory guidance is provided by ARB 43, (codification No. 330) and IFRS guidance is outlined in IAS 2, *Inventories*. Both US GAAP and IFRS provide guidelines for valuation adjustments and cost flow assumptions.

Valuation adjustments include the lower-of-cost-or-market adjustment which ensures that damaged or obsolete inventory is recognized in the period in which value is diminished. Each period, entities determine the market value of inventory, and if the historic cost is greater than current market value entities must write down inventory to its impaired value. Market value is defined as replacement cost with maximum and minimum values. Replacement cost can be no more than the net realizable value (selling price less estimated disposal costs) and no less than net realizable value less estimated normal profit margin.

Under IFRS, impairment of inventory is required; however, there are no ceiling or floor limitations. IFRS could lead to lower quality financials since inventories can be written down below net realizable

---

[61] ARB 43, Chapter 4, ¶3 (Codification 330-10-30).

value less a normal profit margin. When sold, any overestimated loss will be recovered directly into earnings. If the inventory is not sold, but the net realizable value is recovered, IFRS allows for a reversal of the write-down, again into earnings. Under US GAAP, impairment recovery is prohibited unless the inventory is sold above original historic cost.

US GAAP also allows flexibility in assigning inventory costs to expense when the inventory is sold. In a simplistic example, assume that an entity purchases three units of inventory across a year and sells one. If the units are purchased at $100, $110 and $120, the entity must decide which cost is to be assigned to the unit that was sold and expensed to cost of goods sold, and which costs are to be assigned to the two remaining inventory units to remain on the current assets section of the balance sheet. Under a first in first out (FIFO) inventory cost flow assumption, then the cost of the unit sold will be $100 and the two remaining units will have a combined cost of $230. A last in first out (LIFO) cost flow assumption results in an expense of $120 and ending inventory of $210. Note that LIFO minimizes income.

Entities are allowed to use LIFO for tax reporting, but if they do so, they also must use LIFO for financial reporting. Because LIFO results in significantly lower tax payable, entities that benefit from the use of LIFO will presumably continue to do so. Any changes to this rule would need to be enacted by the appropriate US governmental agency. Under IFRS, the LIFO inventory cost flow assumption is not allowed. This area of non-convergence between US GAAP and IFRS is not currently under discussion. Without US governmental intervention to eliminate the conformity rule, US firms will be likely to strongly object to IFRS adoption.

B. Biological assets

IAS 41 defines a biological asset as a living plant or animal. These assets must meet the same general recognition criteria as all other assets, and they are initially recognized at fair value less costs to sell. Since these assets will increase in value as they grow, they are re-measured at each reporting date. In general, biological assets are traded in active markets, and their fair value is determinable. If an entity enters into a futures contract to sell the assets, and losses are expected, the onerous contract provisions of IAS 37 apply.

US GAAP does not specifically identify biological assets, and no specific guidance is provided for these assets. The Codification Industry section No. 905 summarizes guidance for agriculture under US GAAP. As with other items of inventory, animals and crops are held at lower of cost or market or, under certain circumstances, at net realizable value.

C. Plant, property and equipment

Unlike US GAAP, compound assets are recorded under the guidance of IFRS in separate accounts and may be depreciated over different time periods. IAS 16 requires a components approach for capitalization and depreciation. For example, a building may be recorded as the building shell with a 40-year useful life, a roof with a 20-year useful life, and a heating/air conditioning system with a 15-year useful life. Each component is capitalized and depreciated separately, and depreciation is based on the useful life of each individual asset.

Components accounting differs significantly from US GAAP where compound assets may be capitalized and depreciated as one asset. Further differences arise because of impairment rules. Under US GAAP, impairment is required for other than temporary decreases in value, but impairment losses cannot be recovered. Under IFRS, each component can be impaired, and each can be recovered.

Subsequent costs are classified as either replacement of one of the components or repairs and maintenance. If the transaction is considered to be a replacement, then the old asset is derecognized and the new asset is recorded. Repairs and maintenance are expensed. Subsequent measurement under IAS 16 allows assets to be carried at cost, less accumulated depreciation and impairment, or long-lived assets may be revalued to fair value with increases in fair value reflected in equity and decreases in fair value reflected in income. Impairments can be recovered.

Day-to-day servicing costs for PP&E are expensed as incurred, but IAS 16 does not define these costs. IAS 16 does require that recognition be a function of whether there are future economic benefits and that the costs can be measured reliably. Unlike US GAAP, IFRS does not require differentiation of "betterments" from "replacements". Both are capitalized. Under IFRS, an entity must derecognize the component that was replaced.

IFRS seems more transparent in terms of initial asset valuation, but allowing recoveries of impairment may diminish earnings quality compared with the more conservative US GAAP policy of recording impairment only when the impairment is considered to be other than temporary. In such a setting, recovery is not allowed. In addition, IAS 16 requires that each part of an item of PP&E with a cost that is significant in relation to the total cost of the asset be depreciated separately. The judgments required to estimate useful life and salvage value may affect the quality of earnings and the quality of financial presentation.

IFRS allows for a revaluation model to account for PP&E. Under this method, the carrying value for an asset is its fair value at revaluation less subsequent accumulated depreciation and subsequent impairment losses. Revaluations are allowed only for assets that can be reliably measured at fair value. Gains and losses on revaluation are components of comprehensive income.

Interest capitalization (borrowing costs)

Under US GAAP and IFRS, interest cost is capitalizable for all assets that require a period of time to get them ready for their intended use.[62] Qualifying assets include:

(a) assets that are constructed or otherwise produced for an enterprise's own use (including assets constructed or produced for the enterprise by others for which deposits or progress payments have been made);

(b) assets intended for sale or lease that are constructed or otherwise produced as discrete projects (e.g. ships or real estate developments); and

(c) investments (equity, loans, and advances) accounted for by the equity method while the investee has activities in progress necessary to commence its planned principal operations provided that the investee's activities include the use of funds to acquire qualifying assets for its operations.[63]

Inventories are specifically excluded from interest capitalization.

The amount of interest to be capitalized is limited to the actual incurred or the avoidable interest, whichever is less. The avoidable interest is the weighted average interest rate times the weighted average expenditures (or a specific rate, if present). For example, assume that in 20X1, an

---

[62] Financial Accounting Standards Board, Statement of Financial Accounting Standards No. 34, *Capitalization of Interest Cost* (October 1979) [hereinafter FAS 34] ¶8 (Codification 825-20-15).

[63] FAS 34, ¶9 (Codification 825-20-15).

entity constructs a building for its own use. The entity borrows $5,000,000 at 8% for construction purposes. During the first year of construction, the entity makes the following payments related to construction: March 1, $400,000; June 1, $800,000; July 1, $1,400,000 and December 1, $1,600,000. The entity has other debt outstanding, including a 10 year, 10% bond, with a face amount of $5,000,000 that pays interest annually and a 15 year, 11% note, with a face of $2,000,000 and interest payable annually.

Interest capitalization requires the calculation of weighted average accumulated expenditures. The following table provides a schedule of the expenditures weighted by a capitalization period equal to the portion of the year the payment was outstanding.

Figure 9.1: Schedule of weighted average accumulated expenditures and avoidable interest

Date	Construction payment	Capitalization period	Weighted average
March 1, 20X1	$400,000	10/12	$333,333
June 1, 20X1	$800,000	7/12	$466,667
July 1, 20X1	$1,400,000	6/12	$700,000
December 1, 20X1	$1,600,000	1/12	$133,333
Weighted average accumulated expenditures			$1,633,333

Avoidable interest is calculated by multiplying the weighted average accumulated expenditures by either a weighted average of interest rates, or a specific rate, if present. In this example, the total $1,633,333 weighted average accumulated expenditures is less than the construction loan of $5,000,000. The entity should use the 8% interest rate associated with the construction loan to determine its avoidable interest. Avoidable interest is equal to 8% times $1,633,333, or $130,667. The entity must capitalize the lower of the avoidable interest, or the actual interest for the year. Since actual interest equals $1,120,000 (the construction loan of $5,000,000*8% + the bond $5,000,000*10% + the note $2,000,000*11%), the entity should capitalize $130,667 as part of the building account.

If the weighted average accumulated expenditures had exceeded the $5,000,000 construction loan, the entity would have used a weighted average of other interest rates to compute avoidable interest for the excess. In this example, of the additional $7,000,000 in loans, five-sevenths is at 10% and two-sevenths is at 11%. The weighted average is calculated as 5/7*10 + 2/7*11 to yield 10.28%. This is then applied to the excess and added to the avoidable interest of $400,000 already calculated from the construction loan times the construction rate. In deferring this expense, the entity will depreciate it over the estimated useful life of the building.

IAS 23 addresses interest capitalization under IFRS, and defines borrowing costs as interest and other costs that an entity incurs in connection with borrowing. Specifically included are issue costs, bond discounts and call premiums. IFRS specifically excludes borrowing costs related to equity-method investments. Note that substantial differences between US GAAP and IFRS occur in capitalization and impairment of all non-financial assets.

Depreciation

Depreciation allocates the cost of a long-term asset across its estimated useful life. Under the matching principle, the cost of an asset that will be used for longer than one year may not be completely expensed in the year of the asset's purchase. Instead, the cost is allocated across the estimated useful life, and expense is taken each year. Under IFRS, entities are required to capitalize components of PP&E, thus, depreciation is required for each component. Also, as components are replaced, they must be derecognized. Unlike US GAAP, residual values are required to be reviewed at each reporting period.

Under the guidance of IFRS (IAS 5), long-lived assets classified as "held-for-sale" are not depreciated. Instead, they are carried at the lower of their carrying value or their fair value less a cost to sell. Losses are recognized and may be recovered. These assets are listed separately on the balance sheet. In order to be classified as held for sale, management must commit to a plan, the asset must be in sellable condition, management must be actively seeking a buyer, the sale is highly probable within the next 12 months, the sales price is reasonable and the intention to sell is unlikely to be changed or withdrawn.

D. Investment property

Investment property is defined in IAS 40 as property that generates cash flows largely independent of other assets held by an entity. Such property is held for rental or for capital appreciation and not for administrative use or ordinary revenues. Leases qualify for investment property treatment if they are accounted for as a finance lease using the fair value model. Initial measurement for purchased property is at cost while initial measurement for a finance lease is at the lower of the fair value or the present value of the minimum lease payments (see the section on Leased Assets for an explanation).

With limited exceptions, revaluation may be at either fair value or using the cost model. Under the fair value method, the property is measured at fair value each period with gains and losses recognized into income. Depreciation is not charged. Fair value is at an exit price using reliable estimates of comparable value. If fair value is not determinable, entities may use the cost model where the carrying value is cost less accumulated depreciation less accumulated impairment. Assets are derecognized at sale or when retired.

E. Leased assets

Lease accounting provides a striking difference between the standards-based US GAAP approach to accounting and the principles based IFRS model. Under the US GAAP model, leases are capitalized if they meet one of four criteria, otherwise they are considered to be accounted for as rentals. However, application of one provision of the capitalization rules allows lessees to avoid capitalization. Under IFRS, this application is not allowed, thus ensuring that leases transferring risks and rewards of ownership are accounted for as a purchase by the lessee and a sale by the lessor.

Under US GAAP, lease contracts containing any of four specific criteria are to be capitalized. These criteria include:

1   transfer of title;

2   a bargain purchase option;

3   a lease term that equals or exceeds 75% of the economic life of the asset (not applicable in the last 25% of an asset's economic life);

4   recovery of 90% of the fair value of the asset.

Under each of these contractual terms, the risks and rewards of ownership have been transferred to the lessee. While specific criteria exist, closer examination reveals why lessees, under US GAAP, only rarely must capitalize a lease unless it is to their benefit.

Lease contracts can be structured such that the lessor maintains title and offers no bargain purchase option. Thus, the first two criteria can easily be avoided. Since the concept of "economic life" is ill-defined, contracts can be structured to avoid the lease term limitation. Avoiding the recovery test requires slightly more work, but can be structured to be in compliance with US GAAP.

The recovery test states that if the present value of the minimum lease payments equals or exceeds 90% of the fair value of the asset, then the lessee is, in essence, purchasing the asset and should capitalize the lease. There are three important issues associated with this criterion:

1 Computation of any present value requires a discount rate. For lease capitalization, US GAAP requires the use of the lower of the lessor's incremental rate of return or the lessee's incremental borrowing rate.

2 The composition of the minimum lease payments must include the amount to be recovered by the lessor for the cost of the asset, residual values, any penalties for failure to renew and any bargain purchase options. Interestingly, treatment of residual values in the minimum lease payment differs between lessee and lessor depending on whether the residual value is guaranteed.

3 The final issue is that the lessee must capitalize the lower of the present value of the minimum lease payments or the fair value of the asset and recognize a liability equal to the capitalized asset.

For purposes of this discussion, assume the following lease contract. Lessee agrees to lease an asset from lessor for 5 years. The cost of the asset to lessor is $1,000,000. The economic life of the asset is 8 years.

Under the terms of the lease, lessor will maintain title and will not offer a bargain purchase option. Assume that lessor wishes to recover the cost of the asset plus an implicit rate of return equal to 10% and that lessee knows lessor's implicit rate. Lessee's incremental borrowing rate is 12%. Lessor requires a guarantee that the asset's value will be $200,000 at the end of the lease term.

Lessor's required payments to recover the cost of the asset are computed as follows:

Figure 9.2: Lessor's calculations

Fair value of the asset	$1,000,000
Subtract the present value of the residual	$124,184
Lessor's required recovery	$875,816
Factor of annuity due where the term is 5 years and the discount rate is 10%	4.169
Payments (968,954/4.169)	$210,078

With five payments of $210,078, lessor will receive $1,050,390 and the guaranteed residual value of the asset of $124,184 at the end of the lease term. Whether or not the residual is guaranteed, lessor sets payments to exclude the present value of the residual in its minimum lease payments. Lessee, however, includes guaranteed residual values but excludes unguaranteed residual values in calculating minimum lease payments.

Figure 9.3: Lessee's calculations, guaranteed residual value

Rental payments	$875,816
Present value of the guaranteed residual	$124,184
Present value of the minimum lease payments	$1,000,000

Figure 9.4: Lessee's calculations, unguaranteed residual value

Rental payments	$875,816
Unguaranteed residual value	Excluded
Present value of the minimum lease payments	$875,816

The 90% recovery test states that if the present value of the minimum lease payments equals or exceeds 90% of the fair value of the asset, then the lease is capitalized by the lessee. Thus, by not guaranteeing the residual value, lessee falls below the 90% recovery test and is able to treat this lease as an operating lease.

There is no economically sound reason that the lessor would not require some type of guarantee. However, US GAAP allows third-party guarantees to be excluded in the calculation of the lessee's minimum lease payments. The 90% rule also can be circumvented if the lessee does not have knowledge of the lessor's implicit rate, and must use a higher incremental borrowing rate. Under US GAAP, then, lessees are able to relegate lease payments to footnote disclosure and keep substantial debt off-balance-sheet. The effect diminishes the quality of earnings, and depending on the quality of disclosure, may diminish transparency. Under IFRS, third-party guarantees are included in the minimum lease payments of the lessee. Leases that substantially transfer the risks and rewards of ownership are treated in substance as purchases. In the area of leases, IFRS offers a substantively more transparent financial reporting. There are no definitive plans to revisit this issue in the effort toward convergence.

F. Basket purchases and bargain purchases

Entities purchasing more than one asset for a lump sum are said to be making a basket purchase. Asset capitalization in a basket purchase setting may be determined using the relative fair market value method. Under this method, at the time of purchase, each asset is appraised to determine its market value independent of the other assets involved in the transaction. For example, if an entity purchases a new store site including fixtures, a building and inventory, then each asset, including the land upon which the building rests, must be appraised. The assets are capitalized at their relative market values.

For example, assume Smith Company purchases a component of Brown Company, that includes a building, land, fixtures and inventory, for $1,200,000. An independent appraisal determines the following: $500,000 building value, $300,000 land value, $200,000 fixtures value and $400,000 inventory value. Note that Smith is able to purchase the assets for $200,000 less than their independent combined fair market value of $1,400,000. Under IFRS, this transaction represents a bargain purchase and must be examined before proceeding with recognition since bargain purchases may arise from many sources, but one of the most common is measurement error. IFRS 3R requires that before any gains from bargain purchases can be recognized, entities must review valuations. If, after review, a bargain purchase is still in effect, then a gain of $200,000 is immediately recognized.

G. Investments in securities and the equity method

Debt and equity securities that are bought and held principally for the purpose of selling them in the near term are classified as trading securities and reported at fair value, with unrealized gains and losses included in earnings. Debt and equity securities not classified as either held-to-maturity securities or trading securities are classified as available-for-sale securities and reported at fair value, with unrealized gains and losses excluded from earnings and reported in a separate component of shareholders' equity.[64]

Both available for sale and trading securities are "marked to market" at the end of each reporting period. For example, assume on July 1, 20X1, Smith Company purchases 100 shares, which is less than 20% of the total equity of Brown Company, for $100 per share. Smith must classify this investment as either available-for-sale or trading.[65] Under either classification, Smith must determine the share price for Brown at the end of the period, and then adjust the balance sheet account to the new market price. If Brown is $110 per share as of December 31, 20X1, Smith must revalue the asset on its balance sheet to $110 per share. The offsetting of the unrealized holding gain is taken directly to earnings if the security is classified as a trading security, and is reported as a component of comprehensive income if the security is considered to be an available-for-sale security.

---

[64] Financial Accounting Standards Board, Statement of Financial Accounting Standards No. 115, *Accounting for Certain Investments in Debt and Equity Securities* (May 1993) [hereinafter FAS 115] Summary (Codification 320-10).

[65] Equity securities cannot be classified as held-to-maturity by definition.

Entities make their classification choice based on intent and an ability to sell the security in the short term. They may also reclassify the securities. FAS 115 stipulates that: 'The transfer of a security between categories of investments shall be accounted for at fair value.' At the date of the transfer, the security's unrealized holding gain or loss shall be accounted for as follows:

(a) for a security transferred from the trading category, the unrealized holding gain or loss at the date of the transfer will have already been recognized in earnings and shall not be reversed; and

(b) for a security transferred into the trading category, the portion of the unrealized holding gain or loss at the date of the transfer that has not been previously recognized in earnings shall be recognized in earnings immediately.[66]

Reclassification is another tool that has been used to manipulate earnings.

Both US GAAP and IFRS classify Trading or Held-for-Trading securities as short-term investments intended to be held as part of a portfolio with profit-making potential. These securities are reported at fair value with changes taken into current earnings at the end of each period. Under the fair value option (FAS 159 and IAS 39) an entity may designate any financial asset or liability to be measured at fair value when initially recognizing it. Once set, the category cannot be changed.

Entities holding less than 20% of the shares of an investee use the mark-to-market method described above. Entities holding more than 20% of the share of an investee are presumed to have significant influence on that investee and must use the equity method of accounting for the

---

[66] FAS 115, ¶15.

investment. Under the equity method, entities do not revalue the security at the end of the year. Instead, they are required to recognize a proportionate share of the investee's net income or loss. For example, assume that Smith Company holds 25% of the shares of Brown Company and has significant influence. Further assume that Brown reports earnings of $1,000,000 for 20X1. Smith will recognize its 25% share, or $250,000, of Brown's income for into earnings. If Smith is unable to exert significant influence over Brown then Smith accounts for the investment using the cost method fair valued at the end of the period. Unrealized holding gains and losses are recognized into comprehensive income.[67]

APB Opinion No. 18, Interpretation 34 provides examples of indications that an investor may be unable to exercise significant influence over the operating and financial policies of an investee. These include:

(a) opposition by the investee, such as litigation or complaints to governmental regulatory authorities, challenges the investor's ability to exercise significant influence;

(b) the investor and investee sign an agreement under which the investor surrenders significant rights as a shareholder;

(c) majority ownership of the investee is concentrated among a small group of shareholders who operate the investee without regard to the views of the investor;

(d) the investor needs or wants more financial information to apply the equity method than is available to the investee's other

---

[67] This assumes that an entity holding at least 20% of the shares of another entity does not classify that investment as trading.

shareholders (for example, the investor wants quarterly financial information from an investee that publicly reports only annually), tries to obtain that information, and fails;

(e) the investor tries and fails to obtain representation on the investee's board of directors.[68]

Managers have used the flexibility associated with the significant influence rule to manage earnings. IFRS is moving toward the equity method of accounting for similar investments. Thus, transparency will be affected only if IFRS adopts additional disclosure requirements over US GAAP.

H. Asset retirement obligations

Entities must account for tangible long-lived assets that will incur an obligation at retirement of the asset. The guidance in FAS 143, *Accounting for Asset Retirement Obligations*, provides the following:

> This Statement applies to legal obligations associated with the retirement of a tangible long-lived asset that result from the acquisition, construction, or development and (or) the normal operation of a long-lived asset. As used in this Statement, a legal obligation is an obligation that a party is required to settle as a result of an existing or enacted law, statute, ordinance, or written or oral contract or by legal construction of a contract under the doctrine of promissory estoppel.[69] An entity shall

---

[68] Interpretation 35, Criteria for Applying the Equity Method of Accounting for Investments in Common Stock: an interpretation of APB Opinion No. 18 (May 1981) ¶4.

[69] Financial Accounting Standards Board, Statement of Financial Accounting Standards No. 143, *Accounting for Asset Retirement Obligations* (June, 2001) [hereinafter FAS 143] ¶2.

recognize the fair value of a liability for an asset retirement obligation in the period in which it is incurred if a reasonable estimate of fair value can be made. If a reasonable estimate of fair value cannot be made in the period the asset retirement obligation is incurred, the liability shall be recognized when a reasonable estimate of fair value can be made.[70]

In this Statement, the term retirement is defined as the other-than-temporary removal of a long-lived asset from service. That term encompasses sale, abandonment, recycling, or disposal in some other manner. However, it does not encompass the temporary idling of a long-lived asset.[71] The fair value of a liability for an asset retirement obligation is the amount at which that liability could be settled in a current transaction between willing parties, that is, other than in a forced or liquidation transaction. Quoted market prices in active markets are the best evidence of fair value and shall be used as the basis for the measurement, if available. If quoted market prices are not available, the estimate of fair value shall be based on the best information available in the circumstances, including prices for similar liabilities and the results of present value (or other valuation) techniques.[72]

Asset retirement obligations occur when an entity recognizes that it will incur significant costs to retire a long-term tangible asset. Such costs may include site clean-up costs, or land reclamation costs, or any material cost associated with retiring the asset. Entities must estimate

---

[70] FAS 143, ¶3.

[71] FAS143 footnote 2.

[72] FAS 143, ¶7.

the costs related to retirement, and then calculate the present value of these costs. A liability is set up to equal the present value of the retirement obligation, and the long-term asset account is increased by the exact same amount as the liability. The costs associated with retirement obligation, as part of the capitalized long-term asset, are depreciated across the estimated useful life of the asset. The liability remains on the books until the asset is retired. At that point, the actual costs are paid to retire the asset and the liability is removed.

Two other accounting efforts are required for the liability. First, since the liability was recorded initially at its present value, it must be increased for the passage of time.[73] As the liability is increased, an offsetting expense, called an accretion expense, is charged against income. Second, the liability is tested for appropriateness on a timely basis. If the liability account is ever considered to be too low (or too high) in comparison with estimated retirement costs, then the liability is increased (or decreased) along with the capitalized asset account.

Under IFRS, Asset Retirement Obligations fall under the measurement and IAS 37. Unlike US GAAP, capitalization is required if, as a normal policy, an entity believes it is obligated to dismantle and remove the asset and restore the site. Also contrary to US GAAP is the provision that if the risk-adjusted rate changes, then the discount rate used also changes.[74] A significant difference between IFRS and US GAAP occurs with measurement of the liability. Under US GAAP, the liability is required to be measured using an exit value based on externally derived "assumptions about external assumptions." Entity specific estimates are precluded.

---

[73] Since the liability is booked at its present value, the passage of time increases the liability until at the date of retirement; the present value will equal the face amount of the liability.

[74] See IFRIC 1.

Under IFRS, entity-specific estimates are allowed. Under both IFRS and US GAAP, provisions are recognized when the liability is incurred and a reasonable estimate can be made of the amount of the liability. Entity specific values with extensive disclosure of benchmarks may prove more transparent in predicting the actual cash outflows.

I. Intangible assets

Intangible assets are probable future economic benefits that lack physical substance and are not financial instruments. Accounting for intangible assets requires management to judge whether the asset is of indefinite useful life versus limited useful life. Further, the accounting treatment for intangible assets depends upon whether the asset was internally generated, or was purchased.

(a) Purchased intangibles with an indefinite useful life are capitalized, but not amortized. They are subject to annual impairment review and are written down to reflect any decreased value that has occurred.

(b) Purchased intangibles with a limited useful life are amortized across their estimated useful lives. These assets are also subject to impairment review.

(c) Internally generated intangibles with an indefinite useful life are expensed as incurred, as are internally generated intangibles with limited useful lives.

Purchased intangible assets may arise when one entity enters into a business combination with another entity, and purchases the entire entity, not just a component of it. Under the purchase method of accounting for business combinations, the purchaser must determine the assigned value of the identifiable assets of the acquired entity. Purchase price in excess of the assigned value of the identifiable assets is designated as goodwill. Since goodwill is considered to be an intangible asset with an indefinite useful life, it is capitalized, but not amortized to expense on an annual basis. Instead, goodwill, as with all other indefinite-life intangible assets, is examined at least annually to determine if its value has been impaired.[75] If the value of goodwill becomes impaired and the impairment is other than temporary, then goodwill is written-down and an expense will be recorded.

Determination of the value of goodwill is extremely complex. Goodwill is the premium related to projected synergies associated with the purchase of another entity and is represented by the purchase price that cannot be explicitly linked to the assigned value of the acquired entity's assets. Thus, earnings may be managed through judicious allocation of the purchase price to non-wasting assets such as land and goodwill.

Earnings management techniques also include improper classification of other intangible assets, in addition to goodwill, as indefinite-life as opposed to limited life intangible assets. As with goodwill, the costs associated with externally generated, indefinite-life intangible assets are capitalized, but not amortized. These assets are tested for impairment on at least an annual basis; however, their costs are not automatically allocated to expense through amortization. If the externally generated intangible assets are classified as having a limited life, then their costs are amortized (allocated) to expense across their estimated useful lives. As with depreciation, estimating the useful life of the asset presents opportunities for earnings management.

Under the provisions of IAS 38, intangibles are recognized if they arise from legal obligations. Goodwill must be separated into components. Research and development costs under IFRS are required to be

---

[75] The impairment test for goodwill differs from the impairment test for other assets.

separated into a research phase and a development phase. Research costs are always expensed. Development costs can be capitalized if there is a technical feasibility of completing the product, there is an intention to complete the product and either use or sell it, and there must be the ability to use or sell it. This latter requirement may necessitate a market study to confirm usability. In addition, documentation is required to ensure that the asset will produce future economic benefit, and resources exist to complete the product.

Under IFRS[76], impairment of goodwill is tested at the cash-generating unit level, and if impairment losses reduce goodwill to zero, remaining impairment is allocated to other long-lived assets in the cash generating unit on a pro rata basis. Under US GAAP, goodwill is separate from other assets. Another difference arises with recovery of impairment losses. Under IFRS, impairment losses are reversed only if there is a change in estimate used to estimate recovery. Under US GAAP, impairment losses are not reversed.

10. Asset Impairment

Both US GAAP and IFRS require all assets to be tested for impairment if there is an indication that impairment may exist. In determining recoverability, US GAAP allows use of an undiscounted cash flow, while IFRS requires use of a discounted measure. Other differences between IFRS under IAS 36, and US GAAP under FAS 142 and FAS 144, include the grouping of assets to be tested for impairment and measurement of any loss. Under GAAP, grouping is at a higher level, such as asset groups

---

[76] IAS 36.

or reporting units. IFRS allows grouping for cash-generating units. Under GAAP, losses equal the difference between carrying value and fair value, while IFRS determines loss as the difference between carrying value and a recoverable amount defined as the higher of the value in use or fair value less costs to sell.[77] Value in use is generally considered to be the present value of future cash flows including those at disposal. The major differences in IFRS and US GAAP include the timing of impairment tests, the level at which assets are tested, identifying whether impairment has occurred and reversals. Under this provision, IFRS seems more vulnerable to manipulation. There are no current plans for convergence to the guidance provided in IAS 36.

IAS 36 requires a review of all relevant assets at each reporting date. If indicators of impairment exist (such as reduction in the asset's market value or technological changes adversely affecting the asset), IFRS requires calculation of the recoverable amount. If an amount is not recoverable, impairment has occurred. Value in use is an entity specific value reflecting discounted expected cash flows while fair value less costs to sell is an exit value. Value in use is extremely subjective, thus extensive disclosure is required by IAS 36. Normally, value in use would be higher, thus used by the entity, because the value to the entity is greater holding the asset.

Under US GAAP, impairments occur at the "asset group level" while under IAS 36, if an entity cannot identify the recoverable amount of an individual asset, it must calculate the cash generating unit to which the asset belongs. The cash generating unit is the smallest identifiable group of assets that generate inflows. Under IFRS, indefinite life intangibles are tested on an individual basis.

---

[77] IAS 36.

The most substantive difference in US GAAP and IFRS is related to reversals of impairment losses. Under IAS 36, reversals are permitted for all assets except goodwill. After reversals, the new carrying amount cannot exceed depreciated historical cost. Reversals are recognized into income and future depreciation rates must be calculated. Under US GAAP, reversals are not permitted.

11. Liabilities and Contingencies

A. Current liabilities

ARB 43 provides the following:

> The term *current liabilities* is used principally to designate obligations whose liquidation is reasonably expected to require the use of existing resources properly classifiable as current assets, or the creation of other current liabilities.

As a balance-sheet category, the classification is intended to include obligations for items which have entered into the operating cycle, such as payables incurred in the acquisition of materials and supplies to be used in the production of goods or in providing services to be offered for sale, collections received in advance of the delivery of goods or performance of services, and debts which arise from operations directly related to the operating cycle, such as accruals for wages, salaries, commissions, rentals, royalties, and income and other taxes. Other liabilities whose regular and ordinary liquidation is expected to occur within a relatively short period of time, usually 12 months, are also intended for inclusion, such as short-term debts arising from the acquisition of capital assets, serial maturities of long-term obligations, amounts required to be expended within one year under sinking fund provisions, and agency obligations arising from the collection or acceptance of cash or other assets for the account of third persons. The current liability classification is also intended to include obligations that, by their terms, are due on demand or will be due on demand within one year (or operating cycle, if longer) from the balance sheet date, even though liquidation may not be expected within that period. It is also intended to include long-term obligations that are or will be callable by the creditor either because the debtor's violation of a provision of the debt agreement at the balance sheet date makes the obligation callable or because the violation, if not cured within a specified grace period, will make the obligation callable. Accordingly, such callable obligations shall be classified as current liabilities unless one of the following conditions is met:

(a) The creditor has waived or subsequently lost the right to demand repayment for more than one year (or operating cycle, if longer) from the balance sheet date.

(b) For long-term obligations containing a grace period within which the debtor may cure the violation, it is probable that the violation will be cured within that period, thus preventing the obligation from becoming callable.[78]

Proper classification of assets and liabilities as current is vital to decision usefulness and the analysis of liquidity. Working capital, defined as current assets less current liabilities, and the current ratio, defined as current assets divided by current liabilities, provide market participants with information concerning an entity's ability to pay near-term obligations. Misclassification of current liabilities as long-term liabilities

---

[78] ARB 4, ¶7.

does not directly affect earnings, but may reduce the cost of capital by making an entity seem less risky in the short term and may be used to ensure that debt covenants are not violated.

B. Loss contingencies

Loss contingencies are defined as losses that will be incurred contingent upon the occurrence of another event. FAS 5 provides the following:

> For the purpose of this Statement, a contingency is defined as an existing condition, situation, or set of circumstances involving uncertainty as to possible gain (hereinafter a "gain contingency") or loss (hereinafter a "loss contingency") to an enterprise that will ultimately be resolved when one or more future events occur or fail to occur. Resolution of the uncertainty may confirm the acquisition of an asset or the reduction of a liability or the loss or impairment of an asset or the incurrence of a liability.[79]

When a loss contingency exists, the likelihood that the future event or events will confirm the loss or impairment of an asset or the incurrence of a liability can range from probable to remote. This statement uses the terms probable, reasonably possible, and remote to identify three areas within that range, as follows:

1   *Probable.* The future event or events are likely to occur.

2   *Reasonably possible.* The chance of the future event or events occurring is more than remote but less than likely.

3   *Remote.* The chance of the future event or events occurring is slight.

---

[79] Financial Accounting Standards Board, Statement of Financial Accounting Standards No. 5, *Accounting for Contingencies* (July, 1975), paragraph 1.

Examples of loss contingencies include:

(a) collectibility of receivables;

(b) obligations related to product warranties and product defects;

(c) risk of loss or damage of enterprise property by fire, explosion, or other hazards;

(d) threat of expropriation of assets;

(e) pending or threatened litigation;

(f) actual or possible claims and assessments;

(g) risk of loss from catastrophes assumed by property and casualty insurance entities including reinsurance entities;

(h) guarantees of indebtedness of others;

(i) obligations of commercial banks under "standby letters of credit";

(j) agreements to repurchase receivables (or to repurchase the related property) that have been sold.[80]

FAS 5 requires losses to be recognized for loss contingencies if the loss is "probable" and the amount of the loss can be "reasonably estimated".[81] Both of these criteria involve substantive managerial judgment and have been used to manage earnings. Managers wishing to report higher income numbers simply assume that the contingent loss is not probable. For example, entities may consider litigation losses to be less than probable until all legal avenues have been exhausted.[82]

---

[80] FAS 5, ¶3-4.

[81] FAS 5, ¶8.

[82] An entity also may fail to accrue a loss for litigation if it believes that accruing the loss will be considered an admission of guilt.

C. Provisions, contingent liabilities and contingent assets

Under IFRS, provisions, contingent liabilities and contingent assets are defined slightly differently. IAS 37 defines a provision as a liability of uncertain timing or amount. A contingent liability is an uncertain liability or one that is not recognized because it is not probable that it will be settled or it cannot be measured reliably. Contingent assets are similarly defined in terms of uncertain timing and amount under IFRS, but are precluded under US GAAP.

IAS 37 introduces the concepts of provisions, which are slightly different from the US GAAP contingent liabilities. (Current discussions at IASB would replace the term provision with "non-financial liability.") The guidance provided in IAS 37 is not US GAAP and is not part of the convergence project with IAS. Under IAS 37, liabilities are recognized if a legal or constructive obligation exists and a probable outflow can be reliably estimated. (Note that the second criterion that "a probable outflow can be reliably estimated" is expected to be eliminated, which suggests that more liabilities will be recognized under IFRS in the future, and more liabilities will be recognized than under US GAAP.) Under IAS 37, a provision is recognized when a legal obligation exists, which is similar to US GAAP. A striking difference with US GAAP is the requirement that a "constructive" obligation also can lead to recognition.

Constructive obligations differ from legal obligations. Legal obligations result from contracts, legislation or other legal enactments. For example, environmental liabilities are required under various EU directives to be remediated. Under numerous US laws, such liabilities also are legally enforced. Constructive obligations are harder to identify because they result from more subjective conditions. If an entity has established a pattern of behavior that has created a "valid expectation" on the part of a third party that a liability exists, then the entity must recognize the liability. For example, an entity that has paid discretionary bonuses for numerous years may have created an expectation that they will continue to pay such bonuses. In such a setting, if the expectation has been set that a bonus will be paid, the bonus is no longer discretionary and a liability will need to be recognized.

Other differences between IFRS and US GAAP arise when an entity that has contaminated land and faces a legal obligation to remediate the site must recognize a liability under IFRS. Under US GAAP, that entity would fall under the guidance of contingent liabilities and may not be required to recognize a liability if the amount of outflow cannot be estimated.

With extensive footnote disclosure, IFRS would seem to provide more transparent presentation of liabilities. Under US GAAP, contingent liabilities may or may not be recognized; however, under IFRS, even the valid expectation of a liability initiates recognition. Note that contingent liabilities under IFRS are defined differently from contingent liabilities under US GAAP. Under IFRS, contingent liabilities are defined as those which are "possible" obligations (as opposed to IFRS provisions which are "probable" obligations). Under US GAAP, contingent liabilities are recognized if they are both "probable" and can be reasonably estimated.

Measurement of provisions is problematic under IFRS. In general, provisions are measured at the best estimate of the amount required to settle the obligation. The settlement amount is an exit value, thus requires an entity to estimate the costs of transfer or settlement. For some provisions, transfer is impossible. For example, current markets do not exist for transfer of risks, thus measurement of an obligation related to decommissioning a nuclear power plant would be problematic. Entities are required to use their best estimate, but such estimates may reduce transparency of liabilities.

Under IAS 37, measurement is at fair value, which may be estimated using present value techniques. Inflation is accounted for either by using a real (excluding expectation of inflation) discount rate and nominal cash flows (including expectations of inflation) or using a nominal discount rate and real cash flows. Either the discount rate or the nominal flows are adjusted for risk, but not both. Under either alternative, managerial judgment may lead to earnings management or an understatement of the future liability. Without extensive disclosure, transparency may be diminished.

IFRS also requires recognition of onerous contracts in which the costs of meeting the contract are greater than the benefits of the contract. Onerous contracts are recognized as provisions.

12. Pension Obligations and Expenses

Financial reporting of defined benefit pension plans remains one of the least transparent areas in US GAAP. Unfortunately, IASB has adopted guidance which is similar to US GAAP.

In general, pension plans are either defined contribution plans or defined benefit plans. The terms of a defined contribution plan require an employer to pay a fixed contribution into a fund separate from the entity. The employer has no subsequent legal obligation to the covered employees. Under IFRS, a defined benefit plan is one that is not a defined contribution plan. Under a defined benefit plan, the employer promises to pay a fixed benefit at retirement and, in general, the employer has legal obligations to the employee for the duration of the employee's life after retirement.

Not all employees are guaranteed a benefit. Vested employees are entitled to benefits even if they are no longer employed by the firm sponsoring the plan. Non-vested employees are not included in the liability. However, there is a nontrivial probability that non-vested employees will vest. Thus, under US GAAP, alternative measures of the liability include:

(a) *Vested Benefit Obligation* (VBO): The liability associated with vested employees at current salary levels.

(b) *Accumulated Benefit Obligation* (ABO): The liability associated with vested and non-vested employees at current salary levels.

(c) *Projected Benefit Obligation* (PBO): The liability associated with vested and non-vested employees at projected future salary levels.

Both US GAAP and IFRS require the liability associated with the post-retirement benefits of a defined benefit plan to incorporate assumptions about future salary levels and both offer extensive guidance on computing current pension expense. The expense includes:

Service cost

The service cost is the increase in the present value of the benefits due to employee service during the current period. It must be determined by an actuary who is generally an external consultant to the entity. Service costs increase pension expense.

Interest on the liability

Since the current cost is a present value of future benefits to be paid, interest accrues on the obligation. This increase arises because of the deferred nature of pension plans. Interest on the liability increases pension expense.

Expected return on the plan assets

Under both US GAAP and IFRS, expenses are allowed to be reduced by an expectation of return on the plan assets. Since entities are using expectation instead of actual returns, most likely, return will reduce pension expense.

IFRS and US GAAP both adopt the approach that the short-term volatility associated with actual returns should not directly affect earnings. Instead, entities are permitted to subtract expected returns from periodic pension expense, and to consider deviations from the expected return as actuarial gains or losses. This smoothing mechanism can greatly reduce expense since entities are allowed some latitude in their choice of expected rates of return.

For example, assume Smith Company estimates a return of 6% on assets of $1,000,000. At the end of the period, Smith's actual return was $50,000. Smith is allowed to reduce pension expense by the $60,000 estimated return and include the unexpected loss of $10,000 ($60,000 estimated less $50,000 actual) in net unrealized gains and losses to be treated in the same manner as actuarial gains and losses.

Actuarial gains and losses

Differences in the obligation arise due to changes in the composition of the workforce, changes in life expectancy or other changes in actuarially derived estimates. Thus, one component of actuarial gains and losses is associated with the liability. As previously mentioned, differences also arise between expectations of return on plan assets and the actual returns realized on the assets. Both US GAAP and IFRS allow firms to further smooth actuarial gains and losses by subtracting a "corridor" amount, computed as the larger of 10% of the present value of the beginning of the year liability or 10% of the fair value of the plan assets.

Entities may then amortize the remainder over the average remaining service life of the employees or any other reasonable time period.

The corridor approach to pension accounting diminishes transparency. The following exemplifies the corridor approach to pension accounting. Assume Smith Company records the following amounts in its memo accounts at the beginning of 20X4, 20X5 and 20X6:

Figure 12.1: Memo accounts of Smith Company

	20X4	20X5	20X6
Benefit obligation	$210,000	$260,000	$290,000
Plan assets	260,000	280,000	270,000
Unrecognized loss	0	40,000	30,000

The corridor is the larger of 10% of the beginning of the year obligation or 10% of the plan assets. For this example, in 20X4, 20X5 and 20X6 the corridor would be $26,000 (10% of the assets), $28,000 (10% of the assets) and $29,000 (10% of the obligation), respectively. For 20X4, no loss would be amortized since there is no loss in the memo accounts at the beginning of the year. In 20X5, the loss of $40,000 would be reduced by the corridor of $28,000 to yield an unamortized net loss of $12,000. If the average remaining service life of Smith's employees was 6 years, then the loss to be included in pension expense would be $2000. In 20X6, the cumulative loss of $68,000 ($40,000 – $2000 amortization + $30,000) is reduced by the corridor of $29,000 resulting in a net loss of $39,000. If the average remaining service life is now 5 years, the loss to be included in pension expense is $7800. Note the potential for large losses to be greatly reduced by large liabilities.

13. Financial Instruments

Financial instruments are described as contracts that result in a financial asset for one entity, and a financial liability for another entity.[83] IAS 32 provides examples of financial assets and these include cash, equity instruments of another entity or contractual rights to receive cash or to exchange financial assets or financial liabilities.[84] A financial liability is a contractual obligation to deliver cash or to exchange financial assets or liabilities. IFRS and GAAP both require fair valuation of financial assets and liabilities, with gains and losses recognized into income and subsequent remeasurement to fair value for each period. Financial instruments are derecognized upon sale, transfer, or extinguishment of the obligation.

Under IFRS, at initial recognition, financial instruments are classified as:

(a) *Financial assets at fair value through profit and loss*: Instruments classified as fair value through profit and loss are similar to US GAAP trading securities. These instruments are held with a view toward selling in the near term. When held as part of a portfolio, they are managed for buying and selling with an objective of maximizing profits. Once classified as fair value through profit and loss, securities cannot be reclassified. Revaluation gains and losses are recognized directly into income. Note that these revaluation gains and losses are unrealized holding gains and losses. Thus, initial classification of fair value through profit or loss leads to recognition of unrealized holding gains and losses into income.

---

[83] IAS 32. paragraph 11.

[84] IAS 32, paragraph 11.

(b) *Held to maturity*: Only debt can be held to maturity, and in order to be classified as such, management must demonstrate intent to hold the security until maturity, and the ability to do so. These securities are recognized and held at amortized cost using effective interest amortization, and are not periodically revalued except to impair.

(c) *Loans and receivables*: IFRS classifies loans and receivables as being non-derivative instruments with fixed and determinable payments and not traded in active markets. Loans and receivables are valued as amortized cost using effective interest amortization.

(d) *Available for sale*: Securities classified as available for sale comprise the remainder of financial instruments. If an asset has not been classified as fair value through profit and loss, held to maturity, or loans and receivables, then it must be classified as available for sale. Thus, initial classification as available for sale leads to recognition of unrealized holding gains and losses into other comprehensive income.

Financial instruments may pose classification problems when they contain both debt and equity components. For example, convertible debt may be held or converted into common shares at the option of the holder. Mandatorily redeemable preferred shares are legally considered to be equity, but the mandatory redemption feature is legally enforceable. Such securities should be divided into their debt and equity components.

Accounting for financial instruments can differ significantly under US GAAP and IFRS. Unlisted equity instruments are generally carried at cost under US GAAP, but are measured at fair value under IFRS. Instruments carried at amortized cost using effective interest amortization will differ in determination of the effective interest rate:

calculated based on estimated cash through the expected life of the instrument for IFRS, based on contractual cash flows adjusted for unexpected expected cash flows for US GAAP. Derecognition under US GAAP sets a weaker standard than IFRS, with off-balance-sheet status being easier to achieve. IFRS emphasizes transfer of the risks and rewards of ownership before derecognition, while US GAAP allows for derecognition with substantive risk exposure. Reclassifications into or out of trading status (fair value through profit or loss) are allowed under US GAAP and precluded under IFRS.

Off-balance-sheet financing refers to entity liabilities that are not recorded and thus not recognized on the balance sheet. While these mechanisms are not direct earnings manipulation techniques, they are used to reduce the debt on the balance sheet, which makes an entity seem less risky. Since risk and the cost of capital for debt are positively correlated, a less risky entity pays lower interest rates than a more risky entity. Less risk results in lower interest rates, thus reducing expense. Limitations on off-balance-sheet items under IFRS seems to enhance transparency and quality.

14. Derivatives and Hedging

In general, derivatives are financial instruments that have values which change in response to another or underlying security, require little or no initial investment, and are likely to be settled in the future. Examples of derivatives include forward contracts, in which an entity agrees, for example, to purchase a security at a set point in the future for a set price; and options contracts, in which an entity has the right, for example, to purchase a security at a set point in the future for a set price. Options are rights while forward contracts may be obligations.

Both are considered to be derivatives since their values are derived from the value of the underlying stock. Swaps and futures are different versions of forwards and also qualify as derivatives.

Financial instruments are recognized at fair value. Options are valued using pricing models such as the Black-Scholes model or binomial models. Forwards, futures and swaps are valued such that their values are at the current spot price plus carrying costs. In general, derivatives are recognized as fair value through profit and loss instruments with subsequent measurement holding gains and losses taken through income.

Accounting for derivatives is based on whether the holder is trying to hedge risk or is a speculator engaged in arbitrage. Hedgers, for example, may buy and sell forward contracts to lock in future prices on commodities in order to reduce inventory risk. Arbitrageurs trade in derivatives to earn profits from the trading activity itself. FAS 133, requires that:

(a) derivatives are to be recognized in the financial statements as assets and liabilities;

(b) they are to be reported at fair value;

(c) speculators and arbitragers must recognize gains and losses immediately into income; and

(d) hedgers account for the derivative in alternate ways, based on the type of hedge.[85]

---

[85] Financial Accounting Standards Board, Statement of Financial Accounting Standards No. 133, *Accounting for Derivative Instruments and Hedging Activities* (June, 1998) [hereinafter FAS 133] Summary.

Fair value hedges, in which a derivative is used to offset risk associated with changes in the value of an asset or liability, recognize unrealized holding gains and losses directly into earnings. Cash flow hedges, in which an entity tries to protect itself from variability in future cash flows, recognize unrealized holding gains and losses into comprehensive income.

Derivatives also may be embedded in hybrid instruments. Such instruments may have a non-derivative host contract and an embedded derivative portion. If the host and the derivative can be separated and would be treated as a derivative if stand-alone, the economic characteristics and risks of the derivative are not closely related to the host, and the combined instrument is not being accounted for as fair value through profit or loss, then the embedded derivative must be accounted separately from the host. The most common example of an embedded derivative is convertible debt. The debt instrument is the host, and the option to convert to shares is a derivative to be accounted for as fair value through profit or loss under IFRS and fair value under US GAAP. If the instrument is initially accounted for as fair value through profit or loss, then no bifurcation (separation) is needed. Otherwise, the embedded derivative must be separated from the debt instrument and accounted for at fair value.

Under IFRS, derivatives are initially recognized at fair value, which is composed of the intrinsic value of the derivative and a time value, and they are presented as fair value through profit or loss instruments, thus all unrecognized holding gains and losses are recognized into income. Differences between US GAAP and IFRS accounting for derivatives can affect transparency of financial reporting. In general, US GAAP is considered to be more complex and sometimes more restrictive than the provisions of IAS 39. Yet several instances exist in which IFRS provides the more restrictive guidance.

For example, differences arise with derivatives designated as hedges. Hedge accounting, under IAS 39, is defined as one of three relationships. In a fair value hedge, an entity limits its exposure to changes in the fair value of a recognized asset or liability, or a firm commitment. Cash flow hedges offset exposure related to the cash flows of a recognized asset or liability. Finally, firms may hedge the net investment in foreign operations. Hedges must be documented, must be highly effective and the effectiveness must be reliably measurable.

Guidance for judging hedge effectiveness differs between US GAAP and IFRS. IAS 39, paragraph 9, defines hedge effectiveness as the degree to which changes in the fair value or cash flows of the hedged item that are attributable to a hedged risk are offset by changes in the fair value or cash flows of the hedging instrument. Perfectly hedged items are exactly offset. Under US GAAP, effectiveness is assessed at each reporting period and at least every three months. Under IFRS, effectiveness is required to be assessed only at each reporting period. Entities providing only annual reports must assess effectiveness only on an annual basis. The following examples of other differences are not intended to be comprehensive:

(a) Under US GAAP, entities are allowed to use internal hedges for foreign currency risk while IFRS allows only hedges that involve an external party.

(b) US GAAP allows, under certain circumstances, an entity to use the shortcut method to assume no hedge ineffectiveness, while IFRS requires all hedges to be tested for effectiveness.

(c) IFRS allows partial time period hedging while US GAAP requires the complete time period to the maturity of a financial instrument to be hedged.

(d) US GAAP does not allow interest rate risk hedges in a portfolio of dissimilar assets while IFRS allows this strategy.

(e) IFRS allows foreign currency hedging for commitments to purchase a business while US GAAP specifically precludes this activity from qualifying for hedge treatment.

(f) US GAAP precludes use of synthetic hedges (combinations of derivative and non-derivative financial instruments) while IFRS allows this treatment.

(g) IFRS allows one hedge to offset more than one risk under certain conditions, while US GAAP prohibits this treatment.

Entities also may have contracts that are settled in the entity's own shares. These contracts may be considered derivatives if the contract includes net settlement provisions (settled net in cash or shares). Under IFRS, these contracts are derivatives, are recognized, measured and subsequently measured at fair value with gains and losses recognized into income.

In general, IFRS tends to recognize derivatives at fair value, to remeasure these financial instruments at fair value in subsequent periods, and to take unrealized holding gains and losses into income. IFRS allows riskier strategies and provides fewer rules. Alternately, US GAAP, at one point, provided more than 900 pages of guidance related to derivatives and hedging activities. Critics of US GAAP have used this area to exemplify a rules-based system seemingly out of control. Substantive differences between US GAAP and IFRS remain to be resolved.

15. In Process Research and Development (IPRD)

FAS 141 R (effective on or after 15 December 2008; codification number has not been assigned) and IFRS 3R recognize in-process R&D as an intangible asset if there is control over future economic benefits through a contract or other legal mechanisms or if the intangible asset is separable, regardless of whether the holder intends to sell or transfer the asset. The effect on transparency and quality is difficult to judge. There will always be divergent opinions on the effect of IPRD depending on its initial allocation.

16. Share Based Payments

Equity instruments may be used as considerations in transactions. Share based payments may result from options plans to employees, business combinations where shares are issued in payment and certain circumstances where shares are used to pay for services. Accounting for these payments depends on whether the transaction is settled with equity, cash or a choice of the two. If the transaction is settled with equity, then the entity receiving goods and services credits an equity account. If the transaction is settled with cash, then at recognition, the transaction is credited to a liability account. If a choice of settlement methods exists, then the terms of the option determine how the transaction is recorded.

Transactions which are settled in equity are generally measured at the fair value of the goods or services received. Under IFRS, exceptions exist for services provided by employees where it may be difficult to determine the value of the services. In this setting, measurement is determined by the fair value of the equity instruments. If the transaction will eventually be settled in cash, a liability is recognized for the fair value of the liability at the grant date or the date that the entity receives goods or services. Liabilities are remeasured at every reporting date.

Transactions in which there is a choice of settlement are recognized depending on which party has the option to choose the settlement method. If the entity providing goods or services has the option to choose settlement in either equity or cash, then the entity receiving goods and services may need to recognize a liability or a compound instrument containing a liability. Compound instruments require allocations to debt and equity components. Allocations to equity are measured as the difference between the total transaction value and the fair value of the debt component. If the entity receiving goods and services has the choice, then the entity determines whether it must record a liability. If the entity has a history of settling such transactions in cash, then a liability exists.

Employee options for equity pose a greater measurement problem. In this setting, the option on the share must be valued and if a market price does not exist, an options pricing model, such as the Black-Scholes model, is used to determine compensation expense. Substantive managerial judgment is required in model estimation of expense, and even though disclosure is required, transparency may not be achieved.

While differences exist between US GAAP and IFRS in tax treatment of share-based payments, in general, the US had adopted the fair value provisions of IFRS. On the whole, both methods require that all share-based payments be recognized at fair value, with expense recognized when goods are received or services have been rendered.

17. Restructuring

Under the provisions of FAS 146 (Codification 420-10-25-1), a liability for a cost associated with an exit or disposal activity is recognized and measured initially at its fair value in the period in which the liability is incurred.[86] The fair value is computed as the present value on the date the liability is established. Thus, disposal activities generate expected costs, the costs are recognized at the present value of the future amounts to be paid and the related liability must be reviewed on a periodic basis and adjusted if found to be materially different from what is expected to actually occur.

IFRS requirements for restructuring are provided in IAS 37, and restructuring provisions are required only if an entity has committed to the restructuring task. Unlike FAS 146, an entity must demonstrate implementation. Liabilities are recognized if the obligation for restructuring arises from a detailed formal plan that identifies the business part to be restructured, its locations disclosed, explicit definitions of employees to be compensated for termination, and specific identification of implementation procedures. Current discussions suggest that IFRS will yield to US GAAP as provided in FAS 146, thus reducing transparency in the intent to restructure.

Under IAS 37, the restructuring plan must identify the businesses affected, their locations, the location and function of the employees who will be compensated for termination of their services, the expenditures expected to be undertaken and the approximate date the

---

[86] Financial Accounting Standards Board, Statement of Financial Accounting Standards No. 146, *Accounting for Costs Associated with Exit or Disposal Activities* (June 2002) [hereinafter FAS 146] ¶ 3, (Codification 420-10).

plan will be implemented. An entity must raise a valid expectation that it plans to restructure, and it must communicate the plan to its affected employees.

Prior to the issuance of FAS 146, US GAAP allowed great latitude in accruing restructuring charges. Certain entities tended to overestimate restructuring costs then accrue losses with related liabilities. When actual losses were revealed to be less than estimates, the "gains" were taken to income. Additionally, restructuring was often used to hide ordinary losses. With the adoption of FAS 146, restructuring anomalies are much less problematic. Convergence to IAS 37 will help differentiate valid restructuring activities from ordinary business losses.

18. Business Combinations

Both US GAAP and IFRS have been revised with convergence as a guiding principle; however, accounting for business combinations has not fully converged. Under both methods, an acquirer is identified, goodwill is recognized, and non-controlling interests are specifically acknowledged. Under the acquisition method, the acquirer, or party that gains control, must revalue and recognize assets and assume liabilities of the acquired entity at the acquisition date. The assets and liabilities of the acquirer that existed at the date of acquisition are maintained at their existing carrying amounts. Non-controlling interests remain with equity holders who were not part of the purchase agreement.

In general, at the acquisition date, the acquirer recognizes and measures the identifiable assets and assumed liabilities at fair value of the acquiree. Acquisition price above the fair value of the identifiable assets and liabilities indicates goodwill, and a price below fair value indicates badwill or a bargain purchase. Considerations that are contingent at the acquisition date are remeasured at each reporting period with gains and losses reported through income. Goodwill is recognized as an intangible asset. It is initially measured as the cost in excess of the fair value of identifiable assets, liabilities and contingent considerations. Badwill also is recognized, but only after it is reassessed to confirm its existence. If, after careful review, badwill is shown to exist, it is immediately recognized into income.

Both US GAAP and IFRS require acquisition related costs, such as legal, accounting and valuation fees, to be treated as period costs and immediately expensed. Both sets of guidance require contingent considerations to be revalued after acquisition dates and subsequent gains and losses recognized into income. Differences exist between US GAAP and IFRS in treatment of non-controlling interests. These interests can be measured at fair value, or may be measured at the proportionate share of identifiable net assets, under IFRS; but are measured only at fair value under US GAAP.

A. Consolidated or separate presentation

Under IFRS, the degree of ownership interest determines whether financial statements are consolidated or presented separately. Investments with no control or significant influence are presented separately, while investments in which the investor gains significant influence must be accounted for under the equity method. Under IFRS, investments with joint control may be accounted for using either the equity method or proportionate consolidation, while US GAAP generally does not allow proportionate consolidation.

Control generally assumes that one entity has the power to set policies and to benefit from activities of combined entities. Entities with more than a majority of voting power are assumed to be in control of the combined entity. Other indicators of control include the ability to appoint or remove the majority of board members, or the control of board voting power. In general, under both US GAAP and IFRS, control leads to full consolidation. IFRS does allow exemption from consolidation if the parent is a wholly-owned subsidiary of another entity (or partially owned and the other owners do not object), or the parent does not have publicly traded debt or equity, or the parent is private. US GAAP does not allow exemptions from consolidated reporting.

If control is lacking, then under IFRS, investments in subsidiaries, jointly controlled entities and associates not "held-for-sale" are accounted for at cost or as financial instruments recognized and subsequently remeasured at fair value. Under US GAAP, either the cost or equity method is allowed, depending on the degree of significant influence.

The equity method is required for investments in which the investor has significant influence over the investee. Under both US GAAP and IFRS, the presumption is that ownership between 20% and 50% yields significant influence. Under the equity method, initial investment is recognized at cost in an asset account. Cash dividends or other distributions received from the investee reduce the investment account, while recognition of investor's proportional share of investee's income increases the account. Adjustments to investor's shares of income include depreciation based on investee asset fair value and impairment of implied goodwill. Under IFRS, accounting policies between investor and investee must be the same, while they are allowed to differ under US GAAP.

19. Income Taxes

In many areas, US GAAP accounting and the Tax Code differ. In some instances, such as the LIFO conformity rule, entities must use the same methods for tax and shareholder reporting. In other areas, such as recognition of the interest on tax-exempt investments or warranty expense recognition, entities are precluded from using the same methods for external financial reporting that they use for tax reporting. Differences may be permanent, such as recognizing tax-exempt income for external financial reporting purposes. Alternately, differences may simply be timing differences in which a revenue or expense item is recognized during one period for external financial reporting purposes and during a different period for tax reporting purposes. Entities with timing differences will establish asset or liability accounts to reconcile the differences between tax expense (external financial reporting amounts) and tax payable (the actual dollars paid to the Treasury). These differences result in deferred tax assets and liabilities.

A deferred tax asset is recognized for temporary differences that will result in deductible amounts in future years and for carryforwards. For example, a temporary difference is created between the reported amount and the tax basis of a liability for estimated expenses if, for tax purposes, those estimated expenses are not deductible until a future year. Settlement of that liability will result in tax deductions in future years, and a deferred tax asset is recognized in the current year for the reduction in taxes payable in future years.[87] For example, assume that Smith Company, in its first year of operations, estimates total warranty expense for its 20X1 sales to be $100,000. The entire warranty expense

---

[87] Financial Accounting Standards Board, Statement of Financial Accounting Standards No. 109, *Accounting for Income Taxes* (February, 1992) Summary, [hereinafter FAS 109].

is recognized in 20X1 for financial reporting purposes. However, the tax code precludes recognition until the warranty expenditures are actually paid in labor or additional inventory to replace defective products. If Smith actually pays $40,000 in warranty labor in 20X1, then at a tax rate of 40%, a difference of $60,000 (40% of the $60,000 difference) will exist between tax expense and tax payable. This amount will be used to establish a deferred tax asset account. Under US GAAP, deferred tax assets must be adjusted by a valuation account if, more likely than not (a greater than 50% chance), some portion of the deferred tax asset will not be recognized. The valuation adjustment is offset with increased tax expense for the period. For both US GAAP and IFRS, deferred tax assets are recognized for tax loss carryforwards.

Deferred tax liabilities result from temporary differences that result in future taxes. For example, an entity accelerating depreciation for tax purposes may report straight line depreciation in their financial statements. Income will be higher for shareholder reporting (resulting in higher tax expense) while the tax shield is in effect and will be lower than treasury reporting (tax payable) once the shield has expired.

For example, assume Smith Company capitalizes a component of an asset for $100,000 on 1/1/20X1. For financial reporting purposes, the component is depreciated over 5 years and Smith estimates there will be no salvage value. For tax purposes, the component is mandated to be depreciated over 3 years expensing $40,000 in 20X1, $30,000 in 20X2 and $30,000 in 20X3. For computational ease, assume that revenues are $100,000 per year, depreciation is the only expense for Smith, and that the tax rate for financial reporting purposes is 50%. The following tables provide income for financial reporting and treasury reporting purposes.

Figure 19.1: Income for financial reporting

	20X1	20X2	20X3	20X4	20X5
Revenues	$100,000	$100,000	$100,000	$100,000	$100,000
Depreciation	20,000	20,000	20,000	20,000	20,000
Pre-tax income	80,000	80,000	80,000	80,000	80,000
Tax expense	40,000	40,000	40,000	40,000	40,000
Income	$40,000	$40,000	$40,000	$40,000	$40,000

Figure 19.2: Income for treasury reporting

	20X1	20X2	20X3	20X4	20X5
Revenues	$100,000	$100,000	$100,000	$100,000	$100,000
Depreciation	40,000	30,000	30,000	Shield expired	Shield expired
Pre-tax income	60,000	70,000	70,000	100,000	100,000
Tax payable	30,000	35,000	35,000	50,000	50,000
Income	$30,000	$35,000	$35,000	$50,000	$50,000

Figure 19.3: Smith's entries

	20X1	20X2	20X3	20X4	20X5
Tax expense (debit)	$40,000	$40,000	$40,000	$40,000	$40,000
Tax payable (credit)	30,000	35,000	35,000	50,000	50,000
Deferred tax liability (credit)	10,000	5,000	5,000		
Deferred tax liability (debit)				10,000	10,000

In the first three years, the liability is originated and is recognized as the difference between the expense and the payable. During origination, the expense for financial reporting purposes is greater than the cash outflow to the Treasury. In years four and five, the tax shield has expired, and all income is subject to the 50% tax rate. The liability is drawn down by the difference between the expense and the payable, and at the end of year five, the deferred tax liability has been reduced to zero.

The tax expense has a current and non-current component and these are recognized into income except in situations where the underlying taxable event is recognized into comprehensive income, or the tax arises from a business combination. US GAAP and IFRS do not contain fundamental differences in recognition of deferred tax assets and liabilities, although IFRS does not address the uncertain tax position guidance offered by FIN 48, *Accounting for Uncertainty in Income Taxes*. IFRS also precludes valuation adjustments to the deferred tax asset and does not allow separation of deferred tax assets and liabilities into current and non-current portions (all are presented net and considered to be non-current). IFRS requires extensive disclosure about the components of tax and any unrecognized amounts.

Part Four

First Time Adoption: IFRS 1

Coventry University
Lanchester Library
Tel 02476 887575

Borrowed Items 27/02/2013 16:56
XXXX-XX9230

Item Title	Due Date
38001005623933 Modern financial managemen	11/03/2013
38001005031996 Management and cost accoun	11/03/2013
38001005350766 Corporate finance	11/03/2013
38001005879980 * Transparency in financial re	20/03/2013

* Indicates items borrowed today
Thankyou
www.coventry.ac.uk

The SEC's roadmap is controversial and convergence to IFRS may not be as secure as once thought. The current roadmap allows the largest US entities to begin IFRS reporting in 2009, with large accelerated filers following in 2014, other accelerated filers in 2015 and full convergence in 2016. Each entity would need to report three years of US GAAP comparables in addition to full IFRS statements. While full adoption depends on meeting a series of milestones, full convergence to fair valuation, especially in non-functioning markets, is unpopular in the US. To the extent that convergence is a political issue fully supported only by an administration no longer in power, convergence in 2016 may be an optimistic projection.

Opponents suggest that such an aggressive timetable, especially with global recession, could lead to disastrous results for the US economy. They suggest the major culprit is fair valuation, especially with Level 3 inputs in unstable markets. Other opponents have suggested that IASB's recent capitulation on fair valuation for banks in the EU implies that carve-outs will seriously erode comparability, the central reason given in support of convergence.

FASB and IASB continue to converge individual standards, which may make the convergence roadmap irrelevant. The two regulatory bodies have indicated their wish to converge standards related to revenue recognition, financial statement presentation, consolidations, financial instruments and other reporting issues. Such a case-by-case scenario for adopting almost identical standards reaffirms the belief that US GAAP and IFRS will ultimately be strikingly similar, but not identical.

The SEC's roadmap does allow for early adoption of IFRS, thus discussion of IFRS 1, *First Time Adoption of International Financial Reporting Standards*, is useful for US GAAP entities who would benefit from convergence.

IFRS 1 provides guidance for first time adopters and requires that entities:

(a) make an explicit statement of compliance with IFRS, presumably to reduce the number of carve-outs;

(b) comply retrospectively with the IFRS in effect at their conversion date;

(c) recognize the assets and liabilities measured at fair value as required by IFRS, and must remove assets and liabilities disallowed by the new reporting standards;

(d) prepare an opening balance sheet at the conversion date;

(e) disclose enough information to explain the conversion.

IFRS 1 enforces two general rules. While retrospective application is required, if an entity never collected information initially, relief is granted. Secondly, since the results of accounting estimates from prior periods will already be known at the time of conversion, IFRS precludes use of perfect information. Thus, IFRS 1 contains mandatory and optional exemptions when applying IFRS for the first time. Any adjustments that result from convergence are recognized directly into retained earnings instead of through income.

First time adoption objectives are to ensure transparency, a clear starting point and benefits which will outweigh the costs of conversion. Entities may ignore some transitional rules from other standards if specified by IFRS 1. In general, first time adoption will require an entity to:

(a) Comply with each IFRS standard in effect at the reporting date. For example, if an entity intends to report for fiscal 2014, then data gathering under both IFRS and US GAAP must commence at the beginning of fiscal 2012. Thus, 2012 and 2013 statements are filed under the guidance of US GAAP, and US GAAP and IFRS are both run across 2012 and 2013 to be reported in parallel with IFRS statements in 2014. Under the SEC roadmap, entities will publish IFRS statements in 2014 with US comparatives for 2014, 2013 and 2012 plus quarterly information. Standards must be those in effect at then end of fiscal 2014. This provision may prove difficult since major changes are expected in IFRS between now and the end of fiscal 2014.

(b) Restate all balance sheet accounts to comply with IFRS in effect at the balance sheet reporting date. Entities must recognize all assets and liabilities required by IFRS that have not been required under US GAAP; derecognize all assets and liabilities allowed under US GAAP but disallowed under IFRS; reclassify assets, liabilities and equity under the guidance of IFRS and measure all items using IFRS guidance.

(c) Apply mandatory and optional exemptions.

(d) Reconcile IFRS equity and income with US GAAP.

Restating balance sheet accounts may cause specific problems for US entities, especially those currently using the LIFO inventory cost flow assumption. Note that IFRS does not allow LIFO. Since LIFO is primarily a tax shield, without congressional action, US GAAP entities will experience significant differences in income and cash flows at conversion to IFRS. Use of any other method allowed under IFRS will increase accounting income and income tax. Thus, firms with significant inventory balances using LIFO will likely record increased inventory balances and increased retained earnings (note that changes are recorded into retained earnings and not into current income). Tax payable also will be affected, with a significant cash effect.

20. Asset Differences

The following is not intended to be a comprehensive listing of all asset differences between US GAAP and IFRS. However, entities should carefully consider each of these items in convergence efforts:

(a) Impairment: US GAAP uses undiscounted cash flows to measure impairment losses. IFRS measures impairment based on the higher of the asset's fair value less costs to sell, or the asset's value in use.

(b) Carrying value of non-financial assets: US GAAP determines carrying value based on historical cost less other than temporary impairment. IFRS permits fair valuation with recovery of impairments.

(c) ARO: Discount rates used to determine accretion are based on current market-based rates under IFRS and may be adjusted. Discount rates under US GAAP are set when the liability is recognized.

(d) Borrowing costs: Specific borrowings must be considered in determination of the interest rate, while under US GAAP entities are not required to use all interest rates in determining rates to be applied to avoidable interest.

(e) Leases: All capital leases must be capitalized under IFRS. Under US GAAP, guidance allowing unguaranteed residual values to be excluded from the present value of the minimum lease payments affords considerable latitude in whether or not a liability is recognized.

(f) Biological assets: Under IFRS, all biological assets are to be measured at their fair value. US GAAP recognizes these assets at cost.

(g) Investment property: US GAAP has not required separate classification of investment property. At first time adoption, this asset will require separate recognition.

(h) Financial asset derecognition: US GAAP allows off-balance-sheet classification, while IFRS will allow fewer instances to be off-balance-sheet. Previous transfers under US GAAP may require reversal.

(i) Unlisted equity securities: These securities have been carried at cost under US GAAP. Under IFRS, unlisted equity securities will need to be reclassified as available-for-sale financial instruments, and must be carried at fair value.

(j) Differing definitions: The word "probable" in determining accrued continent liabilities will result in recognition of liabilities under IFRS that had not been recognized under US GAAP. Under US GAAP "probable" has been interpreted at a level much higher than the 50% "more likely than not" interpretation found in IFRS.

(k) Contingent liabilities: Contingencies are accrued at the low end of a range under US GAAP while they are measured at the mid-point for IFRS.

(l) Restructuring provisions: Provisions, in general, are more likely under IFRS compared to US GAAP. Under US GAAP, restructuring accruals are allowed only if the restructuring plan has been communicated to the affected employees.

(m) Onerous contracts: IFRS requires recognition as provisions while US GAAP only recognizes limited instances of onerous contracts.

21. Mandatory and Optional Exemptions

To ease transition, IFRS 1 allows mandatory and optional exemptions for first time adopters. Adopting a new set of standards will provide entities with the opportunity to review their financial reporting processes. In some instances, entities will be offered the option of a clean slate.

A. Mandatory exemptions

Derecognition of financial instruments

Entities are prohibited from applying the derecognition requirements of IAS 39 to transactions occurring before January 1, 2004. If a transitioning entity derecognized non-derivative financial assets or liabilities under US GAAP for a transaction occurring before January 1, 2004, then IFRS prohibits recognizing these non-derivative instruments at implementation unless the information needed for recognition was obtained at the initial date of recognition. Entities may derecognize financial assets or liabilities under the provisions of IAS 39 if the information was obtained at the initial recognition dates.

Hedge accounting

Hedging guidance is to be applied from the date of transition forward. Entities are prohibited from declaring a hedging relationship retrospectively. If an entity had designated a hedge that no longer qualifies under IAS 39, then that hedge must be discontinued.

Estimates

Entities are not allowed to use hindsight in making estimates for opening balance sheet measurement. Entities are required to use estimates made under previous US GAAP unless there is evidence of an error. If an entity must revise estimates to comply with IFRS, then the estimate must reflect conditions in effect at the date of transition.

Assets classified as held for sale and discontinued operations

While IFRS 1 labels this guidance as a mandatory exception, it is not. Instead, the exception noted in IFRS 1 nullifies an exception from IFRS 5. Thus, the IFRS 1 mandatory exception requires compliance with IFRS 5 from the date of transition.

Non-controlling interests

From the date of transition, entities are required to split comprehensive income between parent and non-controlling interests; to account for changes in ownership interests and to account for loss of control. Since FAS 160 addresses these issues, this exemption should not be problematic for US GAAP adopters.

B. Optional exemptions

These exemptions arise from guidance provided in other IFRS materials. They are optional at initial transition to IFRS. They include:

Business combinations

Most entities transitioning into IFRS will not have collected sufficient information about past transactions to fully implement IFRS. Entities are allowed to maintain prior business combinations under non-IFRS guidance or to choose a date from which they will begin applying IFRS to past transactions. If an entity elects to use non-IFRS guidance for the business combination, it must ensure that other guidance under IFRS is being met (unless specifically excluded). For example, an operating lease under US GAAP that requires capitalization under IFRS would need to be treated as a capital lease. Although the business combination is exempt from restatement, the assets and liabilities of the acquired entity are not, unless specifically excluded under the provisions of IFRS 1.

Fair value or revaluation as deemed cost

IFRS allows each class of PP&E to be measured at cost or revaluation. At transition, an entity must choose one of these methods and must apply it prospectively. The clean slate aspects of using fair value as deemed cost are cost beneficial, but may cause transparency problems. Entities are required to disclose the aggregate of fair values as deemed cost and the aggregate adjustment to previous carrying values under US GAAP.

Employee benefits

This provision of IFRS 1 is already converged with US GAAP. Under this provision, entities not recognizing unrealized actuarial gains and losses are allowed to recognize the cumulative amount at transition and use the corridor approach for all future expense determination. Since US GAAP already requires the corridor approach, no action will be required.

Cumulative translation differences

Transitioning entities are allowed to ignore application of IAS 21 if they set cumulative translation differences for all foreign operations at the date of transition to zero and exclude translation differences that arose before the transition date from future disposal gains or losses on foreign operations.

Compound financial instruments

Transitioning firms are not required to split compound instruments if the liability component is no longer outstanding.

Assets and liabilities of subsidiaries, associates and joint ventures

Transitioning entities are allowed to use deemed cost of either fair value or carrying value under previous GAAP to measure initial cost of investments. A subsidiary that transitions at a later date than its parent may use its own transition date or based on numbers in effect at that date in the consolidated financial statements.

Designation of previously recognized financial instruments

At transition, an entity may elect to designate any financial asset or liability as fair value through profit or loss if it meets the fair value requirements of IAS 39. Entities must disclose the instrument's fair value, carrying value under US GAAP and classification under US GAAP.

C. Other adoption considerations

Entities must anticipate legal, tax, human resources and information technology issues. The documentation requirements of SOX 404 will affect internal control testing. Covenants, contract provisions, compensation plans, asset valuations, key performance indicators, internal reporting systems, analyst information and local tax reporting must all be reviewed to ensure compliance with IFRS. As the convergence planning stages commence, entities should ensure that accounting, financial and information technology resources are in place and trained in IFRS.

Risks associated with conversion

Transition to IFRS will be lengthy and expensive for US GAAP entities. The following issues should be under current examination by US GAAP entities to ensure a smoother transition to the new standards:

(a) Failure to have sufficient and sufficiently trained staff to effect the conversion is likely the most risky aspect of convergence. Retention of key employees and judicious hiring of IFRS educated staff is essential to a smooth transition. While consultants serve a useful purpose, they cannot know an entity's business model as well as staff. Key staff will ensure that timetables are met, standards are applied consistently and fatigue associated with this extremely large project is minimized.

(b) Maintaining communications with board members, staff, audit committees, analysts and other stakeholders is crucial to convergence success. Management also may wish to educate these stakeholders about the volatility effects of fair valuation.

(c) Training should begin several years in advance of convergence. Managers who may not be technically proficient must be trained concerning the tangential effects of conversion. While most colleges and universities are incorporating IFRS into their curriculum, additional technical training will be required for all staff.

(d) Management must continue to monitor internal control and must be prepared to certify effectiveness of processes.

(e) IT systems must be capable of handling the conversion process. Data collection and disclosure are greatly enhanced under IFRS and IT should be involved in the conversion from the onset of planning.

Coventry University Library

Conclusion

The plan to adopt IFRS in the US is a controversial one. Although early feedback on convergence was positive, more recent developments have raised considerable concerns about the fair value provisions of IFRS. Early advocates of convergence pointed to the significant growth and acceptance of IFRS in most countries around the world. With its perceived reduced complexity, IFRS was viewed as the solution to voluminous guidance offered by the US. More recent concerns focus on the complexity inherent in fair valuation and the lack of convergence on major issues between US GAAP and IFRS. Lack of convergence on major issues such as LIFO make early adoption a risky proposition.

Transparency may improve with adoption of IFRS. However, convergence of US GAAP and IFRS is not guaranteed to improve the quality of corporate earnings and financial reporting. To the extent that fair value becomes just another method used to mislead investors and creditors, adoption of IFRS will lead to serious financial reporting issues. The factors that led to increasingly complex guidance under US GAAP will not go away.

Evidence suggests that carve-outs will continue to exist, even if the US adopts IFRS as its financial reporting basis. For example, in early 2009, FASB adopted a weakened fair value provision for valuing toxic assets in illiquid markets, resulting in a windfall for banks' first quarter earnings. In a shift away from the strict fair value interpretations of IFRS, FASB rushed through a provision allowing entity-specific models to value such assets, instead of market models. Under Congressional pressure, FASB carved-out a provision central to IFRS, which will allow US entities to use questionable numbers in valuing assets and reporting earnings. The IASB rejected FASB's softening of fair value guidance, suggesting that FASB's rush to change the rules is piecemeal and has not been thoroughly studied. Most certainly, the real victim of adopting carve-outs under political pressure is investor confidence in the transparency of financial reporting.

Bibliography

Articles

Bellovary, Jodi L., Giacomino, Don E. and Akers, Michael D., "Earnings Quality: It's Time to Measure and Report", www.nysscpa.org/cpajournal/2005/1105/essentials/p32.htm.

Black, Fischer and Scholes, Myron, "The Pricing of Options and Corporate Liabilities", *The Journal of Political Economy* 81:3 (May-June 1973), pp. 637-654.

Comiskey, E. E., McEwen, R. A. and Mulford, C. "A Test of Pro Forma Consolidation of Finance Subsidiaries" *Financial Management* 24 (1987), pp. 45-50.

Deloitte & Touche, *Quality of Earnings* (2002).

Hirst, D. E. and Hopkins, P. E., "Comprehensive income reporting and analysts' valuation judgments", *Journal of Accounting Research* 36, Supplement (1998), pp. 47-75.

Hodge, Frank, "Investors' Perceptions of Earnings Quality, Auditor Independence, and the Usefulness of Audited Financial Information", *Accounting Horizons* 17, Supplement (2003), pp. 37-48.

Hopkins, P. E., "The effect of financial statement classification of hybrid financial instruments on financial analysts' stock price judgments" *Journal of Accounting Research* 34, Supplement (1996), pp. 33-50.

Hunton, J. E. and McEwen, R. A. "An assessment of the relation between analysts' earnings forecast accuracy, motivational incentives, and cognitive information search strategy" *The Accounting Review* 72 (October 1997), pp. 497-516.

Hunton, J., Libby, R., Mazza, C., "Financial reporting transparency and earnings management" *The Accounting Review* 81, pp. 135-157.

McEwen, R. A., Hoey, T., and Brozovsky, J., "Codification: A Crucial Step Toward Simplification" *Accounting Horizons*, 20:4 (2006), pp. 391-398.

McInnes, M., and Cataldo, J., "SFAS 159: The Fair Value Option", *The CPA Journal*, August 2007, http://findarticles.com/p/articles/mi_qa5346/is_200708/ai_n21293122/pg_1.

Maines, L. and McDaniel, L. "Effects of Comprehensive-Income Characteristics on Nonprofessional Investors' Judgments: The Role of Financial-Statement Presentation Format" *Accounting Review* 75:2 (2000), pp. 179-207.

Penman, Stephen H., "The Quality of Financial Statements: Perspectives from the Recent Stock Market Bubble", *Accounting Horizons* 17, Supplement (2003), pp. 77-96.

Richardson, Scott, "Earnings Quality and Short Sellers", *Accounting Horizons* 17, Supplement (2003), pp. 49-61.

Schipper, Katherine and Vincent, Linda, "Earnings Quality", *Accounting Horizons* 17, Supplement (2003), pp. 97-110.

Websites

www.eifrs.iasb.org

www.fmcenter.aicpa.org

www.investopedia.com

www.ratefinancials.com

Index

A

accumulated benefit obligation (ABO) 87

AICPA, see 'American Institute of Certified Public Accountants'

American Institute of Certified Public Accountants (AICPA) 5

asset(s)

> biological 26, 27, 56, 59, 112
>
> capital 80
>
> differences, between IFRS and US GAAP 112-113
>
> financial 8, 31, 71, 90, 113, 114, 117
>
> impairment 38, 59, 60, 63, 65, 76, 77, 78-80, 82, 102, 112
>
> intangible 7, 26, 27, 56, 76-78, 97, 101
>
> leased 65-69
>
> non-current 36, 56, 57
>
> non-financial 8, 63, 112
>
> retirement obligations 9, 73, 74, 75

B

balance sheet xi, 20, 25, 26-28, 58, 64, 70, 92, 110, 111, 113, 129

bargain purchases 65, 66, 67, 101

basket purchases 69

bill-and-hold sales 47-49

Black-Scholes-Merton formula 7

Black-Scholes model 12, 13, 93, 98

business combinations 76, 96, 97, 100-102, 115

C

capital 11, 14, 28, 38-39, 52

capital lease 112, 116

carve-outs 18, 21, 25, 37, 41, 109, 110, 121

Cataldo, James 14

code law 17-18

codification 6, 18, 19-20

common law 17-18

comprehensive income 25, 26, 30-36, 41, 61, 70

G

H

hedging 31, 92-96, 114

I

IAS 1 *Presentation of Financial Statements* 26, 27, 30, 38, 40

IAS 2 *Inventories* 57

IAS 7 *Statement of Cash Flows* 56

IAS 11 *Construction Contracts* 52

IAS 12 *Income Taxes* 27, 28

IAS 16 *Property, Plant and Equipment* 31, 59, 60

IAS 18 *Revenue* 6, 44, 45, 52

IAS 19 *Employee Benefits* 31

IAS 21 *The Effects of Changes in Foreign Exchange Rates* 31, 116

IAS 23 *Borrowing Costs* 63

IAS 32 *Financial Statements: Presentation* 40, 90

IAS 33 *Earnings per Share* 19, 32, 33

IAS 36 *Impairment of Assets* 78, 79, 80

IAS 37 *Provisions, Contingent Liabilities and Contingent Assets* 59, 75, 84, 86, 99, 100

IAS 38 *Intangible Assets* 31, 77

IAS 39 *Financial Instruments: Recognition and Measurement* 31, 71, 94, 95, 114, 117

IAS 40 *Investment Property* 64

IAS 41 *Agriculture* 59

IFRS 1 *First-time Adoption of IFRS* 109-118

IFRS 3R *Business Combinations* 10, 69, 97

IFRS 5 *Non-current Assets Held for Sale and Discontinued Operations* 28, 115

income statement 4, 25, 28-29, 33, 37, 41

income taxes 31, 103-106, 111

inputs 7-11, 13, 41, 109

intangible asset(s) 7, 26, 27, 56, 76-78, 97, 101

interest capitalization 61, 62, 63

interim reporting 37

inventory 57-58, 93, 104, 111

investment property 26, 27, 57, 64-65, 113